A Documented Biography of Jesus Before Christianity

A Documented Biography of Jesus Before Christianity

ABRAM EPSTEIN

A DOCUMENTED BIOGRAPHY OF
JESUS BEFORE CHRISTIANITY

iUniverse books may be ordered through booksellers or by contacting:

iUniverse
1663 Liberty Drive
Bloomington, IN 47403
www.iuniverse.com
1-800-Authors (1-800-288-4677)

ISBN: 978-1-4917-7507-3 (sc)
ISBN: 978-1-4917-7508-0 (hc)
ISBN: 978-1-4917-7506-6 (e)

Library of Congress Control Number: 2015913153

Print information available on the last page.

iUniverse rev. date: 10/23/2015

CONTENTS

DEDICATION

This work is dedicated to my aunt, Lottie Ganz, who has been gone from this world too long. Her presence still sits across from me at the small, round pine table where we spent many hours philosophizing. Thank you, Lottie for teaching me that the most courageous mind must risk doubt to see the color grey on God's palette. I will always picture you standing in awe of the sky on a rainy day.

PREFACE

When a Christian scholar writes about Moses, or a Jew about Jesus, I believe we may have some explaining to do. Because my intention has never been to dismantle anybody's religious beliefs, offering a few words about the genesis of my thesis seems appropriate.

As those who join in prayer on Rosh ha-shannah and Yom Kippur know, we Jews ask God "al tikach ruach kodshecha mimenu." Do not take Your holy spirit from us. Like most Jews, I had given the nomenclature little extra thought, until, years ago, when I first became aware of its pronounced importance throughout the Hebrew Bible. There, in many of scripture's most illustrious passages, it is exalted as a principle of human interaction with God. Further confronted by its continuing spiritual dimension in the Dead Sea Scrolls (see Thanksgiving Hymn 15) I had come to realize the holy spirit is, in fact, a Jewish concept at the heart of God's relationship with the creation, imbuing worthy recipients with a transcendent awareness of God's will.

How had it been lost as a Jewish interface with God after Jesus' death?

Following Jesus' demise, Jews of the first centuries chose to relinquish their spiritual emphasis on the holy spirit rather than be mistaken for advocates of Christianity. More than a doctrinal component of the Trinity, the fledgling church had made it a steppingstone from "parochial" Judaism to the "new time" of universal inclusion of gentiles and proselytes in the religion's proposed kingdom under Christ.

From my perspective, if Jesus was attempting to restore his ignorant disciples to their Hebrew family with words of Torah, believing the commandments were imbued with ruach ha-kodesh (the holy spirit) his aspiration, owing to their ignorance, may have been futile–but his goal was steeped in the deepest Jewish tradition. Therefore, given his was the voice of a profound Jewish spirituality of the first century, I could not fathom why he was vilified, arrested and put to death. It made no sense.

Determined to know why he suffered so grim a fate–and to find and return the lost Jewish spirituality executed with him, I set out on this intellectual journey. After two years of graduate research for a leading scholar, while attending New York University's Hagop Kevorkian Center for Near Eastern Studies, I became aware of the many profound issues hovering over New Testament studies. Perhaps most provocative, although least often verbalized, was the question of how Jesus saw himself–and whether he believed he was anointed by God as the messiah. Dating back to the late 1700's almost all serious scholars, of whom the majority were Christian theologians, had recognized the Gospel passages in which Jesus asserted his messiahship were editorial enhancements. Further, it was generally conceded he had never promulgated the model of salvation theology which we know–and his devotees formulated postmortem–as Christianity. Naturally, Jesus' reticence about his divine identity and mission might have threatened faith in him, had not that very faith become the precondition of salvation according to the church–and that included justifying his grim demise as God's plan.

Almost of equal weight as an incendiary question was what Jesus had done to be arrested. (Indeed, notable theologians had asked the same question as I more than a century earlier.) Other rabbis of his era had made themselves conspicuous as healers with messianic powers, but at most only bore the brunt of popular mockery, not suffering official sanction or the unimaginably gruesome punishment of crucifixion.

Attempting to fill the void of Jesus' own silence on the subject of his divine identity, while proffering notions concerning his divinely "orchestrated" arrest, many works have since the mid-1800's been written, intending to dispel doubt with verbal acrobatics demonstrating his supra-human attributes. Their argument amounts to saying Jesus' ability to do miracles proves he didn't have to die—and his life's end was therefore a Divine plan.

Such portraits have failed to render a three-dimensional, recognizable Jesus whose life was more than the sum of teachings, miracles, healings, confrontations, persecution and suffering. Somehow, even the most rigorous critical efforts to dislodge and separate theological enhancement in the Gospel text from historically authentic events have produced little more than misshapen or two-dimensional characterizations, so that Jesus has been variously depicted as a rebel, religious reformer, magician, stoic Greek-style philosopher, prophet—and even a con artist duping the people to believe he was the messiah.

All such works have been largely based on the subjective impressions and, often, religious agenda, of their authors.

More worthy of respect, in the course of the past century, scholars seeking to discern stylistic textual patterns and content-related indications of historicity have generated a large following. For example, since 1900, it was recognized that the Gospels of Matthew and Luke had much in common with Mark—but had other content in common with each other that was not in Mark—and an array of scholars postulated the existence of a never-found proto-source labelled "Quelle"(German: "source")— suggesting it was a lost Greek version of Jesus' aphoristic teachings. Indeed, the tidal flow of such efforts still rises.

As a point of information and without any wish at aggrandizement, *A Documented Biography of Jesus Before Christianity* claims an accomplishment New Testament scholars have considered impossible. Rudolph Bultmann, the 1920's originator of the influential two-source hypothesis, declared a genuine pre-Christian biography of Jesus could never be written—that it was simply inaccessible from the accounts of the Gospels. With the publication of this work, he is proven unequivocally wrong.

As I fully elaborate in the Introduction, my own study depends on an altogether new approach. Conceptually, it is similar to the style of argument befitting a court of law—with at least two verifying "witnesses" (that is, segments of Gospel text) establishing the veracity of the case being made. Based on multiple passages supporting an assertion that a biographical event actually occurred, I link it to consequences (that is, other events) which may also be supported as biographically certain based on the evidence of obscure text becoming contextually clear and persuasive for the first time.

Both in method and substance, then, this study has no parallel. Delving beneath the enhancements, miracles and theologizing layers of the Gospel text, *A Documented Biography of Jesus...* penetrates the exegetical gloss to reach the historical core, fully illuminating the epic drama of Jesus' life and death for the first time.

Whereas I have attempted to accommodate both lay and scholarly readership throughout, Part I may rightly arouse mild impatience by establishing method, background and context of the drama about to unfold before advancing to Part II, the biography itself. Please begin with Part II if that is your preference.

INTRODUCTION

Jesus, at the age of just twenty-six, though some thought he was a few years older, had begun teaching a small group of fishermen from Beit Zaida, a village on the north side of the Sea of Galilee. Exactly what excited his students' interest in learning Jewish traditions, Temple culture and synagogue prayer, is fairly certain: The new year Rosh hashannah, autumn of 31CE was approaching, when anticipation was in the air. The "shemitah" as it was called, the revered seventh year of the tithing cycle, was a time for new beginnings when the land would rest from harvests, and there would be an end to binding each other with oaths and debt. A topic of religious and national importance in every Judean home, it was a year many prayed would witness God's Presence returning to the midst of the People. In 31 CE, the more observant Hebrews harbored hopes beyond the political realm. Not only did they imagine the Romans would be ousted from their Judean occupation by God's messiah, a warrior king from the family of David, but imagined an eternal redemption would be their reward when the great Day of God occurred. Nobody, including Jesus' uneducated acquaintances in the northern Galilee, wished to be left out.

Whatever the circumstances of Jesus' family background (a matter discussed below) Joseph, whom he considered his father until then, had shown him how to read and understand Torah, even having him display his prodigal brilliance to rabbis in the Jerusalem Temple when he turned adult at the traditional 12-year old's ceremony (Luke 2:42-47).

Having matured in his knowledge of Torah and synagogue tradition, Jesus taught his little group, and they were expanded to twelve in number. Other teachers also selected twelve students as an honored circle of disciples (apparently a symbol of reverence for God having kept His Covenant with twelve tribes of Israel). By including his disciples in the Covenanted community of Hebrews, Jesus was paving a path of return–return to the Hebrew community from which their ignorance and indifference had caused them to become socially separated.

As we shall see, understanding their identity as "locals" enduring daily, caste-like, social separation is critical to grasping the consequence Jesus faced by becoming their teacher. Indeed, in the early first century, to be an inhabitant of the Galilee showing no reverence for the Jerusalem Temple, either by making pilgrimages on the festivals (Passover, the Feast of Weeks, the Feast of Booths)–or donating properly cleansed foods for the Priests (Terumah) or the Levites (Tithes), meant one was more than simply "unobservant," or a "sinner." Such a one was considered a doubtful Hebrew by many of the more observant northerners. The concept had at its heart the suspicion that such shortcomings as well as failing to correctly say the Hebrew prayers in the synagogue or keep Shabbat statutes, revealed a family tree possibly contaminated by foreign blood or acts of ancestral incest, rape or adultery. (The evidence that this aspersion was cast against Jesus' disciples is detailed in the main text which follows.)

In the course of this work, we shall see that the northern "Pietists" (an extremist offshoot of the southern Pharisees, documented farther on) comprised the region's supposed Torah authorities. In their adopted roles as such, they defined their own lifestyles as a basis for redemption in the anticipated Kingdom of God.

As the Pietists saw it, for the lineage-contaminated unobservant locals to ever be restored as equal members of the legitimate Hebrew community, it would take decades of Torah study and prayer. Certainly whatever chance the outcasts had of entering God's Kingdom depended on God alone–and was not for them or Jesus to decide.

A strident opponent of their rigid exclusivity, Jesus was a young, brilliant–very Jewish–teacher (rabbi, in Hebrew), who had an altogether different view of his students than did the Pietists. Certainly, he fully grasped that they had little familiarity with the spiritual bond-to-God conceptualized in the Hebrew Covenant. But Jesus believed if he could teach them to express their devotion to God through synagogue prayer, excursions/pilgrimages to the Jerusalem Temple, and observance of at least the main Torah commandments, his students like other Jews, might be welcomed into the coming Kingdom, even if it commenced on that very Rosh ha-shannah of 31CE. Though the subject requires full explication, which it receives farther on, suffice it to note, Jesus placed his faith in God's spirit as the means which would inspire his uneducated students. Enabled by the "ruach ha-kodesh," the holy spirit, those with "ears to hear" would grasp and become devotees of central Torah concepts. Such was the teaching of the Jewish sages, manifest in the doctrine of Torah and the prophets and emulated by Jesus in hopes of restoring his disciples to the community of Hebrews.

As the evidence will show, his efforts hardly played out as he expected. At the outset, the Pietists regarded his behaving toward a group of questionable Hebrews as if they were a legitimate circle of rabbinic disciples to be contrary to Jewish norms.

His "healings" added to the rumors and suspicion that he believed he had messianic authority. When Jesus did exactly what other young rabbis did (as he himself says, Matthew 12:27), setting an example of offering sick people hope that they might recover–his students boasted of his success, their proud exaggerations telling of cures of protracted and even lifelong conditions considered possible punishment by God (see healing of the leper, Mark 1:40-1:44), amounting to supposed forgiveness of the afflicted individual's sin.

As ill will spread among Pietists, local lakeside synagogues were abuzz with stories that he even performed healings on Shabbat when congregants solicited his touch and blessing–as if he were master over Torah law.

Most dramatic were the attempts to cure the mentally ill of what were popularly perceived as demons. People acting "crazy" or "out of their minds" were millenia away from Freud and terms like "psychosis." Possession was therefore the usual diagnosis, and treatment, generally, the rabbi's province–since a demon was in satan's cohort, and divine intercession might win the reprieve of the individual's soul. Among those exorcisms attributed to Jesus, one which is historically authentic (see, Exorcism at Kfar Nahum, below), would prove devastating to his reputation.

Frustrated by persistent rumors he claimed messianic powers, Jesus rebuked his disciples' exaggerated reverence, a constant refrain which led to their whispering about the great secret of his identity, only to be revealed to the worthy when the time was right.

Still, none of these factors led directly to his crucifixion, and that story is best told with due attention to the conflicting personalities and religious perspectives just preceding the actual drama.

The method of analysis used in this study

Finding the historical core in the Gospels' midrashim

The use of "lesson-legends" to amplify and interpret religious truths was a deeply-rooted literary technique of the ancient rabbis. Such legends embellished and dramatized episodes described in the Torah (giving them an extra aura of divine intention) and authoring them was a standard practice in Jesus' era. The Hebrew name for them, *midrashim,* meant made-up stories which interpret the meaning of presumed actual events. In the early centuries of our era, such dramatic, theological enhancement through legends was never created from "whole cloth," but consisted of fancifully embroidering events considered historical, with their imaginative elaboration built on the supposed actual occurrences. Therefore, one may say, a *midrash* always had at its core an event regarded by its author as historically true.

Christianity's most famous candidates include (all references are provided along with discussion of the passages): Jesus being born from a virgin, his healing incurable diseases, turning water to wine; Jesus contemplating the adulteress brought before him for judgment, his temptation by satan on the Jerusalem precipice, walking on water, calming the storm, feeding thousands from a small basket of food, and giving Peter the keys to the coming Kingdom of God.

Additionally, Jesus' own words were often cloaked in interpretive "midrashic" embellishment, and they too must be the subject of close scrutiny and re-translation in order to unearth what he actually said, and reach the New Testament's historical stratum.

When, like oysters, the Christianizing shells are opened for inspection, the startling drama of Jesus' life emerges as the "pearls" of history are strung together.

The reader should be aware that *midrashic* analysis is not the same as searching out a natural explanation for seeming miracles. For example, others have suggested that the "miracle of feeding a multitude from a few loaves" may be explained by a storage facility for baked goods to which Jesus had access. Attempting to reduce the "miracles" to mundane episodes by guessing at "plausible explanations" is a false step obfuscating what actually occurred. To speculate in such a manner is to further gloss and conceal the interconnected sequence of unfolding occurrences, burying the actual history beneath the description.

The *midrashim,* it should be stated, differ from parables–*meshalim*– which do not have a historical core.

Meshalim–are short stories with a lesson meant to interpret or explain a higher moral truth, generally embodied in a scriptural passage. Usually called "parables," many of those in the Gospels were authored by Jesus himself, while others were not. Because those spoken by Jesus are a window into his teaching, examining them is of immeasurable value.

A number of other doctrinal warning parables, though authored postmortem, are also of pronounced value in recognizing the earliest attempt to construct a salvation theology. Ancillary to Jesus' actual biography, they are briefly considered in Appendix C.

Precipitous insight

In a scientific study, there is, naturally, a laboratory. One can test a theory by recreating the conditions which should cause predictable results, thereby confirming the researcher's hypothesis. Not only can we not subject Jesus, like some readily available chemical compound, to the same conditions of two thousand years ago, but we cannot recreate the conditions themselves, doing only our best to accurately describe them.

Although scholars such as Rudolph Bultmann have made heroic efforts to apply scientific standards to their work, these suffer the flaw of being inductive—that is taking perceived evidence and fashioning truths. This may be compared to putting together pieces of a jigsaw puzzle with no resulting picture, or one that is utterly deformed.

Fortunately, there is another scientific model for New Testament studies besides laboratory replication, or arriving at a composite portrait formed by ill-conceived, intuited suppositions.

It is the model of "precipitous insight." In application, it depends on the concept of clarification.

To wit: If an insight into an event in the Gospels is capable of dramatically clarifying thematic and linguistic uncertainties found elsewhere in the text, the insight, called "precipitous," is elevated to the level of hypothesis. As hypothesis, it may be "tested" by its predicted consequences. If, for example, it links to other text, creating further pronounced insight, the exponential increase in clarity is likely an advance toward a unified theory.

Here is an example: Jesus conducts an exorcism of a man in the Kfar Nahum synagogue after the congregant's demon supposedly screams at him, "I know who you are! The holy one of God. You have come to destroy us!" (Luke 4:31-4:35; Mark 1:21-1:26)

To the traditional Christian, the episode puts Jesus' divine power on display. Historically, however, one may proffer an altogether different viewpoint. Let me suggest this insight: The congregant, a normal man who had heard rumors that Jesus was evil, actually omitted "The holy one of God" and really said, "I know who you are! You have come to destroy us!" referring to upstanding Jews like himself. "The holy one of God" is deleted as a midrashic embellishment.

If so, the congregant, despite his crazed appearance, was not considered possessed by his fellow-congregants and Jesus, making the mistake of thinking him mad, had silenced a devout, normal Jew.

This interpretation is scientifically supportable only if there are related Gospel texts which, once obscure, are now clarified. Indeed, in Nazareth we have a direct reference to "what you did in Kfar Nahum" (Luke 4:23-24; hypothetically silencing a devout Jew and revealing himself, in so doing, to be evil). When Jesus responds, saying "Satan would not cast out satan! If he did his kingdom would not stand!"(Matthew 12:26) we now grasp the explicit reference to Kfar Nahum—and the entire sequence of Jesus being thought satanic emerges. As the following discussions shall show in due course, the clarification resulting from the Kfar Nahum insight is exponential—clarifying and illuminating much thematic syntax of Jesus' travail, long lost to obscurity, and now retrieved.

Insights into Gospel midrashic text may be derived linguistically, or through textual analysis, or by interpretation of substantive elements. But the veracity of any proposed insight is doubtful if it conflicts with the contextual clarification emerging from the method.

An example: One cannot correctly propose that Jesus envisioned and taught an end to Torah would be accomplished with his death and resurrection if, absent midrashic enhancement, his words indicate he believed Torah's sanctity was eternal.

It also must be acknowledged that in some instances a Gospel insight may clarify a subsequent episode (such as the wedding of Cana clarifies the identity of the woman caught committing adultery) without that second episode lending itself to further clarification of other obscure Gospel text. Her identity, while a persuasive hypothesis, must therefore be labelled informed conjecture.

Background history of the early decades of the first century: The players and the play—the stage is set

In the early part of the first century, during the reign of the Roman emperor Augustus (27 BCE to 14 CE), Judea had been reduced from an independent principality to a province of Rome. Herod the Great, who died in 4 BCE, bequeathed his rule to his son, Archelaus, but it was not Rome's inclination to trust the whole region to a new king of the Jews. Instead, they gave him the title, "Ethnarch," and divided the country into three regions, giving his other sons, Antipas and Philip, jurisdiction as "tetrarchs" over the north, including the Galilee, and areas east of the Jordan River.

When Augustus died in 14 CE, he was succeeded by Tiberius. During his reign, Antipas built the city of Tiberius (about 20 CE), and established a large municipal council as well as a ministerial cabinet. His palatial residence was the site of a scandalous marriage between him and Herodias, the erstwhile wife of his half-brother Philip. Pietists, a Galilee splinter group of extremist Pharisees, abandoned their strict interpretation of legal Jewish divorce to support their adulterous wedlock. They did so because she was a descendant of the Hanukkah-hero Macabees and was eligible to become their longed-for queen. As a reward for their loyalty, many Pietists were included in Antipas' council, enjoying their special title: "Herodians."

In the year six of our era, Augustus banished Archelaus. He was replaced by a Roman governor, Coponious, the first of many. (I should note Pontius Pilate, who ordered Jesus' crucifixion, was governor of Jerusalem twenty years later, from 26 to 36 of our era.)

As a step in asserting Roman governmental intervention in local affairs, the emperor then ordered a census be taken. Its purpose was largely to establish a tax base, but it also had the effect of enrolling Jews as residents of greater Rome.

Very likely at that time, Joseph and Mary made the trip from Nazareth, Antipas' territory (tetrarchy), to Bethlehem to be listed. As the Gospel of Luke states (Luke 2:1-2:20) Jesus was born at the time of the census (about 6 CE).

Priestly sacrifices and festival services, pilgrimages and civil court cases were part of the fabric of social life and were permitted to continue under Jewish auspices with close scrutiny by Roman authorities. Especially significant was the Jewish legislature known as the Sanhedrin. Generally, its members were well-to-do, accomplished men who made civil laws and represented a broad array of constituents. I propose that Joseph was one of them.

Reference to him as such occurs in very early Christian literature (*Protoevangelium of James*) and this matches his financial circumstances. A betrothal to his deceased wife's niece, Mary, when she was only sixteen years old, strongly suggests there was a feduciary component making it a desirable arrangement. His having two homes, one in

Nazareth and the other in the area of Bethlehem, further supplies a portrait of a successful man.

Jesus' last two years–31-32 CE.

The timeframe of his activity

Identified for the first time in this study are the actual seasonal markers, the Hebrew holidays and festivals, which denote phases of Jesus' teaching and healing. Serious attention to their ritual aspects is mostly lost beneath the Gospels' purge of his Jewishness, and a brief survey of them is provided here to illustrate their temporal placement.

In 31 CE

1. The Hebrew festival celebrating both the wheat harvest and receiving the Ten Commandments, called "The Feast of Weeks" or "Shavu'ot" occurs in late May or early June. Jesus teaches the Torah's Ten Commandments.
2. Rosh ha-shannah: the Hebrew New Year is celebrated on the first of Tishrei (about mid-September). Jesus teaches about forgiveness and ending grudges, basic themes of the holiday. Because it commences the Seventh year of the tithing cycle, known as the Shemitah –when all debts are to be forgiven, Jesus spends extra time on the subject of giving charity and correct prayer.
3. Ten days after Rosh ha-shannah: on the Day of Atonement, one confesses to God, and, as Jesus teaches, forgives even those you hate.
4. Five days after the Day of Atonement: during the Feast of Booths (Sukkot) the nation prepares for God's Presence and His coming Kingdom.

Note: Inasmuch as Jesus' "curriculum" focused on restoring the Covenantal equality of his disciples, Sukkot was especially important, prophesied by Zechariah as an envisioned advent of the Kingdom.

5. Hanukkah (Festival of Lights), usually in December. Jesus is nearly stoned for supposedly claiming to be the son of God.

32CE

The continuing timeframe

Winter: John the Baptist is arrested (for saying Herod Antipas' wife, Herodias, is an adulteress). She had never received a legal Jewish divorce.

What may have seemed of little consequence at the time, was the humiliating effect Herodias' marriage to Antipas had on Antipas' other, long-time wife. When Herodias moved in, Phasaelis, as she was called, moved out, fleeing to her father, Aretas, the famed Arab warrior-king of Nabatea.

Aretas threatened to avenge his daughter's humiliation by attacking Antipas. Such was the military and political context which set the stage for John the Baptist's harangues against Antipas, deriding his adulterous union with Herodias and encouraging Judeans to side with the Nabatean, were he actually to do battle (Matthew 14:3-4; Luke 3:19-20). Because the Parthian empire of Persia and the Romans were at each other's throats, Rome simply did not consider Judea's northern region, the Galilee, sufficient concern to preempt an uncertain incursion.

6. Jesus is wary he is being watched. He teaches only in riddle-like parables and does no more healings.
7. Late winter or early spring John is executed: Jesus delivers a eulogy at a large gathering of mourners on the shore of the sea of Galilee. He implicitly derides Antipas' wife for her pseudo-divorce from Antipas' living half-brother Philip. He echoes what John said, and upon learning of his words, Antipas replies he will do to Jesus what he did to John.
8. Jesus is a fugitive.

While it is not the intention of this work to describe the array of characters active in the early post-crucifixion period, one warrants comment: Paul, though he never knew Jesus, lived at the same time. His role, sanctioned by the Jerusalem Center, was to teach gentile communities about Jesus in a fashion consistent with contemporary non-Hebrew beliefs, often at the expense of Torah law. Paul's sometimes contentious arguments with Simon (Peter) are attested in the New Testament, as are his ideas.

Social-religious realities of Jesus' time

Though religious law was the domain of Jewish authorities, the Roman occupation, enforced by considerable numbers of legionnaires, had exacerbated significant disputes among Jews themselves. Worth mentioning, though their role in Jesus' life is unattested, is a group known as Zealot-sicarri who actually engaged in minor revolts and stabbing attacks against Romans, believing God required bloodshed of the occupiers to achieve their withdrawal. On the opposite end of the spectrum, shunning all involvement in political affairs, were the recluse community called "Essenes." Living near the Salt Sea (today known as the "Dead Sea"), their lifestyles are largely known to us from the "Dead Sea Scrolls."

Without doubt, Jesus was not one of them, though this has been postulated because his teaching shared several motifs with theirs.

Other groups endorsed moderate stances toward the Romans, only occasionally reaching the level of active resistance. Best known among these were the Pharisees, a name suggesting their skill in interpreting Torah to make it applicable to daily life.

Identity of the "Pietists"

Some of the more volatile Pharisees had earlier on considered Herod the Great a Roman stooge intent on a proliferation of idolatry. When they tore down a large Roman eagle from the Temple gate, opposing it as idolatrous, many of their number were rounded up and executed. Their group, it appears, subsequently splintered off from the more mainstream Pharisees, and over a period of years, migrated northward, settling in the Galilee, where Jesus taught and lived. In the Talmud (a series of ancient Jewish tracts interpreting, analyzing and explaining Torah law), this offshoot community is characterized as "aping the true Pharisees," always exhibiting their supposed piety as if they were superior to others (Sotah 22a-b).

While apparently keeping the name, "Pharisees," there were a large number who boasted a bloodline from the original Macabee army of "Hasidim," fighting Antiochus two centuries earlier (the Hanukkah War). Therefore, I have labelled the northern extremists, "Pietists," a fair translation of *Hasidim*, in order to show the New Testament reference equating them with the moderate mainstream Pharisees is misleading.

What did these pseudo-Pharisees of Jesus' neighborhood have in common with the more typical Pharisees living in the south and near Jerusalem? There was one abiding, universal belief they shared: God would free the land from Roman occupation and return to the midst of the People, protecting, guiding and loving them as in the days of Moses. It was an ancient idea increasingly the focus of their prayers and rituals, and especially a theme of their home lives. All referred to the return of the Divine Presence as the coming "Kingdom of God." Among their number, many anticipated there would eventually be a great war with a near-magical king, descended from David, to lead them. To some this hope had the character of a legend and would happen in an imaginary future age. To others, the countdown had begun. (The belief in the coming Kingdom of God was a central feature of Jesus' teaching and is discussed farther on.)

Though relatively few in number, other, more superstitious believers influenced by the Salt Sea sect had also introduced the idea that a satanic adversary would attempt to prevent the Kingdom, a villain they named, "the False Teacher." His goal, as an emissary of satan, would be to turn Torah into confused garble, ruining it as a source of God's holy spirit. These various attributes, both for the messianic king and the false teacher created expectations partly responsible for Galilean gossip and rumors about Jesus.

To make the advent of God's Kingdom more immediate, both the Jerusalem Pharisees and Galilean Pietist community borrowed from the tradition of Passover, purifying their houses, and acting like a "Nation of Priests," eating and socially interacting mainly with those who shared their preoccupation.

Any possible defilement of the household environment, each then a model of purity emulating the Temple, was prohibited. Eating with unobservant guests of possibly defiled lineage, including individuals who were considered sinners because they did not adopt stringent rules of cleanliness was frowned upon. Further, if there was evidence of sin, such as adultery, that too was a defilement to be cleansed from their lives.

As noted earlier, ignorance of Torah and Jewish practice was, to the Pietists, a stigma with an especially odious implication. As they saw it, if a local inhabitant didn't know Torah or the correct manner of eating and praying, that person was probably a Hebrew of sinful ancestry. Put simply, although Pharisees to the south were a refined spiritual community, the pseudo-Pharisees of the north, the Pietists, were constantly judging their less observant neighbors as if they were a contaminant society with little hope of entering God's Kingdom.

PART ONE

A. JESUS' JUDAISM

At the outset of Jesus' teaching activity, he engaged in fairly typical and not uncommon acts of compassion toward people who sought the healing touch and blessings of local Galilean rabbis. At twenty-six years of age (though some quoting Luke 3:23 assert he was a bit older), he should not have been more conspicuous than other young rabbis offering similar spiritual therapy—if he had adhered to the interpretations of Torah law demanded by the region's Pietists. But he did not.

Generally, unless an individual's health was a matter of life and death, rabbis refrained from the "work" of healing until Shabbat ended with sundown of the week's seventh day, Roman Saturday, and the new week commenced. Not so, Jesus. In the eyes of synagogue congregants, Jesus' seeming readiness to heal in their sanctuaries on the Shabbat (Sabbath), in what appeared to be blatant disregard of Torah, setting an example to ignorant students, aroused suspicion. His companions, one should note, added to the rumors about his claim to divine authority, inasmuch as they were hardly the usual rabbinic circle. Telling from Jesus' stern correction of their faulty style of prayer, as well as multiple cultural shortcomings (detailed below) the disciples were even considered doubtful Hebrews by many.

Challenged to explain himself, however, Jesus did not say he was above the laws of the Shabbat. Making his point halachically (according to Jewish law) he argued by implication that Torah permitted Shabbat care of hurt animals—and therefore so too, human beings (Matthew 12:11-12:12). "I ask you," he says, "is it not lawful to save life on the

1

Sabbath?" (Luke 6:9). The fact that Pietists had added their own exaggerated rules, as far as Jesus was concerned, was another example of their arrogance. But, healing certain afflictions, whether on Shabbat or any other day, was attended with gossip that he had even claimed authority to cure diseases of "punishment" (lifelong paralysis, leprosy and other chronic, physical maladies), giving solace to several such stricken individuals when they beseeched him for help. (Examples: Mark 1:40-45 healing the leper, Mark 2:3 healing a paralytic, Luke 13:10-13:13 a woman crippled for many years, Luke 6.6 a man with a withered hand, Matthew 15:30-31 healing the blind, lame and mute.)

Assuredly, whatever improvement in their condition resulted, his powerful elixir was more one of faith and hope than medicine. It was an utterly Jewish faith: Adonai would end their suffering. His Kingdom was coming. All would be cleansed of sin, purified and forgiven.

When people–including his own students–began to believe he had divine authority which superseded the Torah's commandments, word spread. Some said that he was God's messiah. Others, like the Pietists and the general Galilean population who heard gossip about Jesus, suspected he was claiming divine authority for a sinister reason. His purpose, they gossiped, was to destroy Torah law. Their evidence? He acted like he alone could heal on Shabbat, and even had God's authority to forgive sin (healing diseases of punishment). As noted, popular rumor had it that Jesus was the one the prophets warned about –the so-called "False Teacher" who would come before the Day of God –when the last battle with satan was to occur. His words, they said, would scramble the very meaning of the Torah's commandments.

His own reaction to being portrayed as the "messianic" Jesus, whether promulgated contemptuously by Pietist adversaries, or from the disciples' reverence, was not a subject he addressed for nearly a full year (summer, 31 CE until spring, 32 CE). As this study will show, Jesus did not realize his students were seriously propagating the messianic rumors by boasting about his "powers." Perhaps, overhearing them express exaggerated boasts about him to Pietists, he may have enjoyed getting "under the skin" of those so irritated by any hint he had divine authority. Beyond conjecture, one may state with certainty, the disciples had an altogether different perception of the future than Jesus had promised. Whereas his goal was to enable his students to appreciate Torah, learn to pray properly, participate in the Jerusalem Temple culture–and be Covenantally restored as righteous Hebrews returned to the fold–theirs was to gain an eternal foothold in God's coming Kingdom and exercise authority over those who had made them outcasts. Ironically, as we shall see, as the April (Nisan) of 32CE approached, circumstances changed and he fully grasped the extent and impending consequence of his disciple-promoted, messianized stature. But the danger to his life, stemming from an altogether unanticipated adversary, abetted by his own disciples, was a fire burning out of control.

The central theme of Jesus' teaching:

Though Jesus taught about specific Jewish rituals (enumerated below), I suggest he focused on those most relevant to spiritual preparation for God's coming Kingdom. Aware that he was teaching things virtually foreign to his students, Jesus was faced with the need to reassure them of their equality with other Jews. Jeremiah, the ancient Hebrew prophet who lived more than six hundred years before Jesus, had promised that the People would one day know Torah in their hearts–and on God's Day nobody would be telling others they were outsiders because they didn't "know about" God.

Echoing the prophet Joel, Jesus believed God's holy spirit was soon to be among the People and everybody, even those considered social outcasts by the Pietists, would be welcome in the Kingdom.

While some have regarded his "curriculum" as a disavowal of the majority of the Torah's commandments, such a view is seriously mistaken. In fact, not once did Jesus disavow anything in the Torah, instead demonstrating his reverence both by inspired interpretations and personal lifestyle.

Before considering the examples of his verbal pedagogy, let us briefly take note of his teaching by example.

Here are various rituals we know Jesus kept, which would have been a model for his disciples to emulate.

A. He was circumcised (this was really a tradition kept by Mary and Joseph) and his disciples knew it–a fact evidenced by its inclusion as a biographical event they later recorded (Luke 2:21).

B. He had a "Bar Mitzvah" (to borrow the anachronistic name of the ceremony from our own time)–though, in those days it was a 12-year-old boy's ceremonial demonstration of Torah knowledge to rabbis (Luke 2:46), a rite of passage commencing adulthood.

C. He kept Jewish dietary laws (later usage: he was "kosher").

There is an edict by the Jerusalem Center (that is, the disciples) instructing Paul to tell the gentile proselytes they may not eat meat of strangled animals or drink the blood of food animals–basic Hebrew dietary laws (very possibly taught them by Jesus) (Acts 15:20). After Jesus' death, Simon (Peter) claims to have received word of a change by authority of a heavenly vision (Acts 11) freeing them to ignore the dietary laws, asserting that from then on everything could be eaten, including items the Torah prohibited as foods. Despite Simon's vision sanctifying a postmortem permissibility to transgress former food restrictions, the fact the Pietists never accused Jesus of such violations indicates he followed the ordinances. In general, the commandments proscribed unhealthy, unclean or naturally deceased animals, those cruelly killed and meat with blood in it. Sea animals without scales and fins (known for unhygienic bottom-feeding) along with predatory wildlife, were also prohibited as was eating a baby animal cooked in its mother's milk. Simon's announced departure from observance of the Torah's dietary laws suggests Jesus had placed little emphasis on them. More than likely this was due to the disciples' main menu of fish and grain, items fully acceptable.

D. He wore Jewish ritual fringes (Greek: cras-ped-on, which those seeking healing touched in Matthew 9:20;14:36). The further, profound implication of such fringes was what wearing them signified: The Torah commanded that they serve as a constant reminder of the commandments (Numbers 15:38).

E. He attended synagogue services on Shabbat.

F. Jesus made pilgrimages to the Jerusalem Temple for the Hebrew festivals.

G. He was skilled in reading from the Torah (actually doing so from the Biblical portion of the prophets) (Luke 4:17).

H. Jesus observed the rituals associated with "shemitah"–the Seventh Year of the tithing cycle (occurring that fateful year, 31-32 CE) and instructed his devotees to end all grudges and debts, exactly as the Torah commanded.

Pedagogy

In addition to setting the "Jewish" example, Jesus not only did not overrule or eviscerate Torah, he exalted it. Here again are a selection of such instances:

I. He taught his students various concepts concerning the Jewish style of prayer, correct behavior in a synagogue, and giving charity (Matthew 6:5-6:8; Luke 6:30).

J. He emphasized the Ten Commandments, reciting them as a lesson (Matthew 19:16-19:20).

K. Much of his teaching concerning prayer and tradition was to enable his disciples to join in observing the Jewish holy days (especially Rosh ha-shannah, the New Year, and Yom Kippur, the Day of Atonement). Because God's Kingdom was anticipated, and considered most likely to occur in the Seventh Year, the disciples' Torah education–and Covenantal identity was all the more important.

L. Jewish instruction using parables were further mainstays of his curriculum.

    1. Repairing their frayed connection to the Covenant, while assuring his disciples of their equality with other Hebrews in the coming Kingdom, was arguably the most compelling purpose of Jesus' teaching.

Perhaps more powerful than any other of Jesus' Jewish themes, therefore, was that concerning Hebrew legitimacy. One surmises he was determined that God's Presence, emanating from Torah would transform his students' lives, purifying their lineages of ancestral sin, restoring them as legitimate members of the Jewish community.

For the Galilean community of observant Jews, and certainly the strict northern Pietists to accept his students as "lineage-pure" Hebrews (that is, having no ancestral origins defiled by forbidden procreation with foreigners, idolators—or descent from incestuous or adulterous union) they would need to "seem" Jewish, keeping the ritual commandments, praying in synagogue, and having some knowledge of Torah. Jesus' reassurance that his students could achieve full equality in the Jewish community reverberates throughout his teaching.

A prime example of a Covenantal restoration parable

[Important note: Jesus was not "Covenanting" individuals whose lineage had fully differentiated them from the Hebrew People. Repeatedly, he emphasizes his efforts are directed to the lost sheep of Israel. Therefore, he extended himself to students whose separateness from the community only faced a barrier of Torah and cultural ignorance. The Pietists might accuse him of offering to Covenant doubtful Hebrews, those whose lineage defilement placed them outside the Hebrew fold—but he would reply that their good deeds proved they came from a "good tree." Therefore, the suggestion Jesus' efforts at Covenantal restoration of doubtful Hebrews was intended also for those Jews spiritually exiled by God, an effort, as it were, to include all devotees in the "saved" community, would be incorrect. "Covenantal restoration," as he indicated, depended on the evidence of a pure family tree, one that was Hebrew and not Gentile.]

"The Prodigal Son"

When it turned out that his disciples were largely disconnected from and ignorant of synagogue culture and Torah, Jesus tried to reassure them they would be equal with other Jews if they "returned to the fold." In the parable of the "Prodigal Son" he compared them to a disloyal son who had strayed from the family and its values (Luke 15:11-15:32). But, as the message clearly implied, if they would return and show their desire to change their ways, they would be especially honored by the family (the Jewish community) and be welcome in the coming Kingdom.

<u>Two other Covenantal restoration parables:</u>

When he was banished from entering the three main lakeside villages, Kfar Nahum, Beit Zaida, and Chorazin (Matthew 11:21) Jesus told the parable about latecomers paid the same wage as those laboring all day in the vineyard. About to bid his students farewell for the foreseeable future (probably, several months, until reunited following John's execution), he wanted them to understand that their recent entry into the "vineyard" (of Torah education) didn't make their value any less than those who entered at an earlier time (Matthew 20:1-20:16).

In still another parable, Jesus taught that God's Kingdom would rise like bread with three measures of flour (the existing society of Hebrews comprising priests, Levites and the mainstream community) mixed with one measure of leaven (!)–an impurity which would become part of the final loaf (Luke 13:20-21). His message was that even if they had impure lineages, his disciples would, like other Jews, be part of the "mix" in the coming Kingdom of God.

2. The second category of Jesus' authentic "instructional parables," is related to the concept of forgiveness.

[Note: Today, "forgiveness" is generally considered a sanctified Christian act. In our own time most of us are familiar with the value Christianity places on forgiving even criminals their wrongdoing (though still requiring their lawful punishment). In fact, Judaism distinguishes between non-criminal and criminal wrongdoings. The only forgiveness a Jew offered another Jew was for non-criminal acts– not murder, or other heinous crimes. In the case of theft, the owner of the stolen goods did have an option to declare them "ownerless" and not press charges. Yet, as this study shows, Jesus' teaching about forgiveness had an altogether different context–a meaning based on Torah tradition.]

When the new year commenced (on "Rosh ha-shannah," the first of the Hebrew month of Tishrei), observant Jews had (and still do) a very strong tradition of forgiving one another whatever grudges they held so that they might ask God's forgiveness without themselves refusing to acquit others. On the seventh year of the tithing cycle, not only were grudges forgiven, but by commandment in the Torah, financial debt was cancelled as well. The Torah was very clear that keeping somebody in financial debt demeaned them as individuals and was identical in its impact to bearing a grudge toward somebody, putting them in your debt until the presumed offense was compensated.

The last months of Jesus' life, extending from Rosh ha-shannah 31 CE until Passover 32, coincided with the sacred Seventh Year of the tithing cycle when all indebtedness–personal grudges and owed money–was to be "forgiven."

If his disciples were to rejoin the fold they would need to understand and behave accordingly.

Here is a brief summary of a premier parable which Jesus used to teach the Torah's commandment to forgive.

Parable of the Unmerciful Servant (Matthew 18:23-35)

A king judged a subject who owed him a large amount of money–saying his punishment would be the enslavement and exile of his entire family until he and they worked off the debt. To this the subject reacted with complete remorse swearing he would repay the money if the king would only have mercy. When the king was moved by his contrition and showed pity totally forgiving his debt, the fellow, nonetheless, revealed his true character, failing to forgive the debt of an acquaintance. Instead, he demanded the jailing of the fellow who owed him far less money than he had owed the king. However, upon learning that the man he had forgiven had not done the same to his fellow man, the king decreed a severe punishment.

The traditional Yom Kippur message was clear: To be forgiven by God—and be worthy of entering the Kingdom —one had to forgive debts and grudges toward acquaintances. Because his disciples could incorrectly think Jesus was teaching from his own "playbook" and mistakenly conclude that the written Torah was secondary or passe (an inclination heightened by illiteracy), Jesus made the unequivocal proclamation: "Anybody who changes even the smallest letter in the Torah will be least in God's coming Kingdom."

Further emphasizing the Torah's commandments, he proclaimed the towering importance "to love God," which Jews then and now recognize to be the heart of Torah, and "to love your neighbor as you love yourself" (Matthew 22:36-40 quoting Deuteronomy 6:5 and Leviticus 19:18).

Though these brief remarks are not the venue for a complete comparison of Jesus' teachings to their Torah sources, one more warrants notation: Instruction to "love one's enemies," and "turn the other cheek" have been mistakenly considered unique to Jesus. In fact, they were typical of rabbinic "fences" protecting and emphasizing the commandment to love your neighbor as yourself. Exodus 23:4 leaves no doubt about the thrust of the commandment. It reads: "If you come on your enemy's ox or donkey going astray, you must lead it back to him... if you see the donkey of a man who hates you fallen under its load...go to him to help him."

M. In his unrelenting effort to encourage his disciples' sense of their Jewish identity, Jesus admonished them not to pray and act like non-Hebrews.

Here is a sample of Jesus' references to the difference between his followers and gentiles:

a. Matthew 5:47 (freely translated): "If you (only) greet each other (and not your fellow-Jews) how are you different from gentiles?
b. Matthew 6:6 "When you pray, do not babble like the gentiles."

    c. Matthew 15:24 "I am here only to teach the lost sheep of the House of Israel."

    d. Matthew 18:17 (freely translated) "(If there is a dispute, and one who is accused refuses to have the matter aired among you) treat that person like a gentile..."

No doubt should exist, therefore, that Jesus was deeply devoted to his own Jewish identity with Torah at its heart. Although early post-crucifixion Christians wanted to dramatize his superiority to Torah, they could not fully delete things various of his disciples knew he had said, or done. (Note: Geza Vermes, too, relies heavily on the contrarian Gospel passages to discern historical authenticity.)

Examples include (freely translated):

    a. I don't want to to abolish Torah...anyone who changes even its smallest letter will be least in God's Kingdom (Matthew 5:17-19).

    b. I am not your judge! (Luke 12:14)

    c. Why do you call me good? Only God is good (Mark 10:18).

    d. If you keep calling me "Lord" I will deny ever having known you! (Luke 13:25-26; Matthew 7:21-23).

    e. Only God knows when the Kingdom will occur (Mark 13:32).

Note: This passage (Mark 13:32) contains the phrase, "not even the Son knows"–a Christianizing insertion which is omitted from Dydimus, and suggests it did not appear even in contemporaneous, unedited editions.

B. THE PIETISTS' JUDAISM

As noted above, traditional Judean Jews of the first century prayed God would again make His Presence felt, as in the days of Moses. According to the tradition, a leader from the lineage of King David would emerge, one blessed by divinely ordained powers to rid the country of its Roman occupiers. This miraculous occurrence was to be "the Day of God" prophesied in earlier times, and the anticipated era was known as "The Kingdom of God."

While the early-to-mid first century Pietists of the Galilee prayed and waited for the Day of God, they focused on maintaining a state of purity both of their household environment and of their personal lives. As they rigorously performed the many commandments of Torah, they believed their worthiness was inviting God to again be in their midst. Because ritual cleansing was a practice of the Pietists and not of the disciples (as we shall see), it played a role in shaping the Pietist perception of them as social outcasts.

Further, by maintaining purity on all levels, the Pietists' lifestyles were a match to the official Temple priesthood. Imagining so special a relationship to God, their self-importance imbued them with a sense of superiority over unobservant northern locals such as Jesus' group. Various of their leaders became members of Herod Antipas' Tiberius council, awarded such positions of administrative power for supporting his adulterous marriage to Herodias. As noted above, we may infer they were the group named "Herodians" in the Gospels.

C. The Disciples: their religious background and relations with the Pietists

Though never actually labeled as such in the New Testament, Jesus' disciples belonged to an established class of regional inhabitants considered "am ha-aretz," a term meaning "people of the land," or more idiomatically, "locals." In the southern part of the country, and among more moderate Jews, it seems the term usually referred to a person ignorant of Torah and purity laws.

Far less vilified, the Jerusalem-area individual, so-labeled, could return to the fold through Torah study and devotion.

A famous example of such an occurrence was that of Rabbi Akiba, who spoke of the time in his early years when he had been an am ha-aretz and hated observant Jews. In his forties, after marriage, he changed and his name today is revered as one of Judaism's greatest Talmudic sages.

The far more parochial northern Pietists, on the other hand, considered the Galilean am ha-aretz to be sinful, possibly lineage-defiled

Hebrews. In their estimation, return was unlikely even if they joined an accepted rabbinic following and dedicated their lives to deep immersion in observing Torah laws for generations.

Reflecting that viewpoint is a quote from the Gospels. In John 7:49-52, the passage quotes Pietists as saying, "This rabble knows nothing about the Law. They are cursed...look into the matter and you will see prophets do not come out of Galilee." (See below for more on the context of this statement.)

Of considerable interest in recognizing the "exilic" character of the northern locals, ostracized by the Pietists as a caste of doubtful Hebrews, is the contemporary account of Yohannan ben Zakkai. It is told that he spent eighteen years living in the Galilee, possibly about the same time as Jesus. While there he was a merchant and also taught Torah, occasionally settling matters of Jewish law brought before him. On one occasion, Yohanan is said to have exclaimed, "O Galilee, Galilee, thou hatest the Torah; hence wilt thou fall into the hands of robbers!"

Not long after, he departed the Galilee and settled in Jerusalem, finally founding the center for Talmudic learning at Yavneh, in the south, where he could presumably be more comfortable among liberal Pharisees like himself.

Returning to his scathing rebuke against Galileans who "hated the Torah" and would "fall into the hands of robbers," one may conjecture he meant the locals, those am ha-aretz cut from the same cloth as Jesus' disciples, seeing they reviled all observance of Torah ritual. In fact, several translations of the Hebrew for Yohanan's "fall into the hands of robbers" (la'assot bamasikin) are possible, including, "you will be besieged." If such was his intended gist, Yohanan may have been referring to the actual history of the north which, according to the Hebrew Bible's record, produced the actual transplanted, non-Hebrew population which became known as the am ha-aretz.

Though scholars do not usually see the Pietists' harsh attitude as a consequence of history, that possibility is worth considering. The Galilee's history did, in fact, establish the origins of the am ha-aretz as lineage-defiled.

In the eighth century BCE, the population extending from Samaria to the northern Galilee, became a mixed population, "polluted" by non-Hebrews brought forcibly to the region. According to Josephus, the first century Jewish historian (Antiquities 9:277-291): "In the seventh year of Hezekiah (Ca. 710 BCE, king of Judah), the Assyrian king Shalmaneser (besieged the capital of the north) and transplanted all its people (the 'Ten Lost Tribes') into Persia...and transplanted other nations into Samaria...and into the country of the Israelites." Josephus further states: "Samaritans, as they were called (after the original northern Israelite capital, Samaria)...brought their own gods into Samaria, and by worshipping them as was the custom in their own countries they provoked almighty God who punished them (with a plague)."

A parallel description is found in the Hebrew Bible (2Kings 17:24-26):

"The king of Assyria brought people from Babylon, Cutha, Avva, Hamath and Sepharvaiim and settled them in the towns of Samaria in place of the Israelites." Friction then developed between the foreigners and those living under Hoshea's Judean reign just to the south of Samaria. The Biblical passage reads: "(They said to the king of Assyria) the nations which you deported and resettled in the towns of Samaria do not know the rules of (our) God."

In the sixth-fifth century BCE, there was further hybridization of the society when Hebrews who returned from Babylonian exile included some already intermarried and others who subsequently married mixed-blood Hebrews, those relocated to the region during the Assyrian conquest of the north, two hundred years earlier.

The Book of Ezra (4) describes their presence, reporting the hostility between them and the Hebrews who refused their participation in rebuilding the Jerusalem Temple: "Thereafter the am ha-aretz (residents of Samaria with foreign ancestry) caused trepidation to the people of Judah and made them afraid...bribing (Persian ministers) to stop them (from the construction of the Temple)."

And Ezra 10:11 states: "[Ezra said to the gathered people, separate yourselves from the People of the Land (am ha-aretz, locals of mixed blood) and from the foreign women."]

Then, from the same historical context, in the Book of Nehemiah (10:31): "We will not give our daughters in marriage to the People of the Land (again, am ha-aretz locals with foreign ancestry) or take their daughters for our sons."

Additionally, in Nehemiah 10:32 the am ha-aretz' indifference to refraining from business on Shabbat is singled out as an example of their conspicuous, sinful lifestyles.

It was this history which may well have lent itself to the especially odious perception of locals in the north.

Whether traced to that earlier history or not, telling from the disciples' unobservant lifestyles, grating dialect, and ignorance of tradition, the Pietists would have shunned Jesus' students for having family histories possibly defiled by sin. Though the earlier era of intermarriage with foreigners is not highlighted in rabbinic texts as a sin transmitted to the first century, such am ha-aretz ancestors, as noted above, were denounced in scripture (Ezra and Nehemiah) for having practiced idolatry. Those scriptural passages were certainly familiar to first century rabbis—as they were to the first century historian, Josephus.

Various passages in the Gospels support the hypothesis that the disciples were castigated for ancestral sin:

In John 7:49-52, the passage quotes Pietists as saying, "This rabble knows nothing about the Law. They are cursed...look into the matter and you will see prophets do not come out of Galilee."

Asked by knowledgeable onlookers, perhaps Pietists, specifically why he ate with sinners (apparently meaning his disciples, Oxyrhynchus Papyrus 1224, fol. 2, verse 2) Jesus replies (//Luke5:30-31):

"It is not the healthy who need a doctor, but the sick" and in Luke 5:32, "I am not (trying to get) the righteous to repent—but to call sinners to repent."

In a transparent attempt to acquit the disciples of being am ha-aretz (and therefore, possibly, lineage-defiled Hebrews) the Gospel formulation has the Pietists ask the disciples (not Jesus himself) why he eats with sinners. Luke, however, preserves the actual exchange by having the Pietists ask Jesus directly, and when Jesus answers, we understand the disciples are the "sinners" in question. The Oxyrhynchus Papyrus supports the Lukan text.

These are remarkable passages for several reasons. First, strikingly, the Pietists considered the unobservant Galilean locals "cursed." What would the curse have been? Most likely, it was spiritual exile by God from the Hebrew People. In other words, their questionable origins had led to possible excommunication by Divine edict—taken almost as fact if they were also blind or lame, or suffered other lifelong maladies considered divine punishment.

Based on the text of Luke 5:32 it seems Jesus too regarded his disciples as am ha-aretz, but in the less harsh sense. His description of them as "sick/sinners" presumes they could be healed by his teaching. To the Pietists, as noted, their lineage defilement would only be purified by generations of obedience to Jewish law.

Further evidence of the disciples' am ha-aretz identity:

As Galileans, Jesus' students comprised "locals," having homes in that region for generations. Mostly making their living from fishing, several lived in the lakeside village of Beit Zaida. Others may have had houses in Kfar Nahum and perhaps Chorazin, also situated on the shore of the Sea of Galilee. The majority being ignorant locals, they matched the am ha-aretz description.

Preserved by the Gospels in detail, Jesus' instruction of the disciples was expansive, supplying us with an accurate tool for measuring their ignorance of Jewish law and tradition. Below, the specific curriculum is outlined, and by inference, we can tell exactly what they didn't know.

Consider several rabbinic statements of the time:

A.

1. "An am ha-aretz is one who prays by babbling like a magician, and knows not what he says" (Sotah 22a).

Comment: In fact, Jesus made a point of telling his adherents not to babble when they prayed, clearly part of his overall effort to free them from the am ha-aretz stigma (Matthew 6:7).

2. "Who is an am ha-aretz? Whoever does not recite the 'shema' morning and evening with its accompanying benedictions" (Sotah 22a).

Comment: The "shema" is a proclamation by Moses found in Deuteronomy, chapter six which translates: "Hear this Israel: Adonai our God, Adonai is the only God." The accompanying benedictions are found in Deuteronomy, chapter 11 and Numbers 15:37-15:41. They call upon the nation to "love Adonai with all your heart, all your soul, and all your might." Contained in the formulation is the commandment conveyed by Moses to repeat the benedictions more than once a day. Thus one who did not say the "shema" was not simply ignorant, but was separated from the religious nexus at the heart of Judaism. Such a deficiency would, as the rabbinic entry above indicates, be a sufficient criterion for attaching the label am ha-aretz to the individual.

Comment: Jesus taught that the shema's commandment to love Adonai was "the greatest commandment" (Matthew 22:37-38). His need to give such instruction was an apparent effort to remove the am ha-aretz stigma.

3. "The sages say: Who is an am ha-aretz? Whoever does not wear fringes on his garments" (Sotah 22a5).

Comment: As we have noted above, Jesus wore fringes. Of importance is the Torah commandment requiring fringes. It may be summarized: "You shall put fringes on the corners of your garments so you will look upon them and remember to keep the laws of Torah" (Numbers 15:39).

Therefore, fringes (Hebrew "tsee-tseet") were actually a way of "wearing" the Torah's laws as a garment.

4. "Who is an am ha-aretz? Whoever has sons and does not raise them to study Torah" (Talmudic excerpt).

Comment: The disciples obviously had never studied Torah, inasmuch as Jesus was teaching them the basics.

B.

The disciples' indifference to physical purity: an am ha-aretz trait

As noted earlier, physical purity had become an obsession with traditional Jews across the land. Waiting expectantly for the miraculous return of God, as in the days of Moses, much of the population prepared by following the example set in that earlier epoch.

In Exodus 19:10-11 God commands Moses, saying, "Go to the People and warn them to stay pure...let them wash their clothes..." to cleanse themselves for the Presence of God.

Observant Jews, north and south, focused on two occasions when purity became a paramount concern, Passover and Sukkot (the Festival of Booths).

Passover was a festival when every home was to be a mini-Temple as the People enacted their role as a "Nation of Priests." It was the only sacred occasion when the non-priestly households sacrificed their lambs, unlike other times when the priests were delegated the task.

Sukkot was the expected occasion of God's return to the midst of the People. As the prophet Zechariah (14:21) had said: "(On that great Sukkot) every metal pot in Judah and Jerusalem shall be holy to the Lord." Purity laws were also emphasized in all matters concerning agricultural produce.

The latter had its own intricate requirements. Outside Jerusalem, individuals partaking in meals from the harvest, had to be certain that the produce had been divided so proper offerings might be sent to the Temple. The allocated portion was either *"terumah,"* a donation to the Jerusalem priests—or was a "tithe" for Levites (Temple administrators with lineage from Moses' tribe). All foods eaten in the Temple precincts, whether by ordinary Israelites or Levites—or Priests, had to be clean. The act of tithing involved certifying the entire source of fruit and grain had not been touched by a list of possible contaminants. These ranged from hands made unclean by contact with dead animals, graves, rotting carcasses, animal blood, and discharges. Any secondary source of contamination, such as dirty clothing, was also kept away from tithes and produce still to be tithed.

Apparently, with the sacred seventh "shemitah" year begun with Rosh ha-shannah 31CE, popular faith in Zechariah's prophesy soared. As many now prayed God would soon return to the midst of the People, northern Pietists became even more rigorous in excluding all sources of contamination, separating themselves from ignorant locals (am ha-aretz neighbors who were unwashed or wore dirty clothing).

Important Gospel evidence of the Pietist viewpoint occurs in Mark 7:1-6 when members of their community challenge Jesus, asking why some of his students eat without washing their hands. Jesus replies, "Yours is the commandment of men" (that is, washing their hands before eating).

He was correct: hand-washing before eating was only required by Torah law: **a.** prior to handling tithes or produce intended for tithing **b.** prior to entering the Jerusalem Temple courtyards and sacred areas **c.** before eating the household festival meals on Passover and Sukkot **d.** before Shabbat meals.

Inasmuch as the role of the Hebrew priesthood (Hebrew: "Kohanim") included acts of healing, purification and cleansing of diseased individuals, as well as determining their right to be included in the community, the Pietists (acting the role of priests) had, without authority, arrogated to themselves the prerogative to distinguish between genuine Jews and those they regarded as having possibly "contaminated" lineages. Their ideas were imbued with a sanctimonious zeal as they waited for God.

Imitating the actual priests, and going even farther, the Galilean Pietists thus saw themselves as adjudicators of Covenantal legitimacy—in other words, judges of who was a true Jew and who was not. Reacting to their arrogance, as the Gospels describe, Jesus repeatedly expressed angry opposition to their self-exaltation accusing them of using ritual to conceal lives of sin—and challenging their knowledge of Torah.

Dismissing the Pietists' claim to "priestly" stature, offended that these pseudo-priests regarded their homes as mini-Temples, and his students as violating laws they had dreamed up, or at least exaggerated, Jesus assailed their own sins as proof of hypocrisy. He was fighting insult with insult. It is interesting to note that he and some of his disciples apparently did wash their hands, and so, escaped criticism. Yet, their motive was not to fulfill a fabricated commandment, as Jesus makes clear, but presumably was simply to be clean. Moreover, his reaction to the Pietists in Mark 7 should not be mistaken for an aversion to Torah law. He was profoundly concerned with washing before entering the Temple precincts, as evidenced by his demand that he and the disciples wash on Passover before the meal—and by his own mikveh – "baptism"– by John on Sukkot. (See a full discussion of the Mark 7 hand-washing episode farther on.)

Before providing further evidence that his disciples belonged to the north's version of the am ha-aretz as a social "caste," completely disenfranchised by the Pietists, let us grasp the significance of their status to Jesus. If, as I shall show, not only they, but their family tree was believed to be possibly sinful, the Pietists would assert that God alone might make them, once again, members of the coming Kingdom. Jesus, by offering them a path to purification, was acting (in the Pietists' view) as one claiming divine authority to forgive their sins and re-Covenant those possibly excommunicated by God. *Not only was his healing of those individuals afflicted by diseases of punishment seen as equating himself with God—but, in all likelihood, so was his claiming the power to Covenantally restore his own disciples—since they were suspected of being cursed by God for sinful ancestry.*

Rabbinic commentary, from the Pietist perspective, adds to the impression Jesus' disciples—as am ha-aretz— would have ultimately required God's own forgiveness.

Mocking the "nature" of the am ha-aretz and by implication derogating their lineage, a talmudic entry states (Sotah 22a, quoting Jeremiah 31:27):

"Concerning him (an am ha-aretz individual) scripture declares, 'I will sow the house of Israel and the house of Judah with the seed of man and with the seed of *beast*'" (my italics). Here we see that the am ha-aretz individual was viewed by some, and certainly by the Pietists, as more like an animal than a human. The reference to "seed" strongly suggests a lineage issue.

Furthermore, marriage to a member of an an am ha-aretz family could produce defiled progeny. In a rabbinic commentary (beraita/ Pesachim 49a) we read: "One should not marry (offspring) of an am ha-aretz. This is like (co-mingling) grapes of a vine with wild grapes of a shrub. It is repulsive and does not yield proper progeny."

In another text from the Bar Kochba era (Ca. 132-135 CE), a passage praises God, stating: "Blessed are You for not having made me a woman, a pagan, or an am ha-aretz." From the viewpoint of the one giving thanks, the spiritual deformity of the am ha-aretz individual was a birth status, not simple ignorance.

Therefore, when Jesus is confronted for having the disciples as his students, he says, "The tree is known by its fruit (Matthew 12:33) and "...a bad tree cannot bear good fruit" (Matthew 7:18//Luke 6:43).

I regard these Gospel quotations of Jesus' opinion to have significance. They stand as proof-texts that the disciples were regarded as lineage-defiled by the Pietists.

Jesus rejects the Pietist view that his disciples are beyond redemption except (perhaps) through generations of Torah study and observance. He responds to the Pietists' mocking criticism, saying that his disciples are righteous and their current good deeds ("fruit") prove their family tree has been restored by God. In saying so, he rejects the notion that every doubtful Jew learning prayer and Torah is forever condemned to exile as one contaminated by centuries of sin.

Quite clearly, even if his disciples are from a doubtful past, Jesus is enabling the return to the Covenantal fold of those Galilean outcasts whose heart is in the right place. As he puts it, they are "the lost sheep of Israel" (Matthew 15:24).

That their doubtful lineage is a salient issue to the Pietists, is further attested in the reference by John when he is immersing northern pilgrims to purify them as they approach the Jerusalem Temple precincts. His words, "God can raise descendants of Abraham from these (Jordan River) rocks," is a reassurance that their pasts can be cleansed whether doubtful or not (Matthew 3:9).

In sum:

We have ascertained that the disciples were mostly uninformed concerning Judaism. Their knowledge of Torah was certainly minimal. To the Pietists, their shortcomings when it came to synagogue culture and ritual participation, taken together with their culturally vacuous lives, were attributes defining them as having possibly sinful or foreign origins. Acting as a pseudo-priesthood the Galilean Pietists therefore treated them as spiritual contaminants exiled from the People by God.

The reader should be aware we are talking about attitudes, not Jewish law. To the Pietists, and to the more extreme members of the Jewish community, the ignorant, unobservant locals were not true Jews–whether that meant due to their sin-tainted family tree, or due to their present revilement of the Torah's commandments.

Either way, their studying Judaism with a teacher suspected of misinterpreting or eliminating commandments according to his own predilection, aroused disapproval; further, Jesus' supposed Covenantal restoration of the disenfranchised "caste of ignoramuses" (the am ha-aretz) generated suspicion he was playing the messiah. As the Pietists saw it, you couldn't restore something that had never been there in the first place. Taken together with the popular notion that the Kingdom of God would occur after a battle between good and evil, the willingness to spread rumors that Jesus was "*the* prophesied false teacher" may not have been widespread, but met no impediment.

Still, it should be emphasized: Despite the disaffection between the Pietists and Jesus, his arrest and crucifixion was, in fact, the result of altogether different events than their contempt for him. Although full explication of their marginal role in his arrest awaits the reader farther on in this analysis, one observation cannot be repeated often enough: The Gospels are clear that no Jew, not even the high priest, Caiaphas, whose perfidy consisted of acquiescence in Jesus' hearing and ultimate execution, *ever* accused Jesus under oath, of claiming to be King of the Jews, or God's anointed messiah. Having no witnesses testifying to his guilt of the capital charge, Caiaphas, nonetheless, accedes to Antipas' demand (detailed, farther on) and hands him over to Pilate for judgment.

D. MATTHIAS, THE TWELFTH DISCIPLE: PROTO-SOURCE

The original Gospel record, deciphered here, was probably kept in approximately the same sequence by Matthias, the twelfth disciple replacing Judas Iscariot, identified just below. Owing to his conjectured role, and occasional mention in this study, a few words about him are appropriate.

[The reader should be aware that although Matthias' newly-recognized prominence is controversial–none of the events described in this study would change were he not the only proto-source. Perhaps he collaborated on an earlier written record with the disciple Philip as suggested by a find in 1952 of the Gnostic Gospel of Thomas which scholars have linked to earlier canonical forms. Because sacred text is often preserved over centuries without losing the value of later versions, one should take note of what Jean Doresse writes (selectively) in "The Discovery of the Nag Hammadi Texts," page 255: "The lost 'Gospel of Matthias,' according to Codex X, is a collection of sacred words written by Matthias which (Jesus) revealed to Matthias in private discourse." The author further observes that Codex X also contains in proximity to the named lost 'Gospel of Matthias,' a Gnostic 'Gospel of Philip' and a 'Gospel of Thomas,' with many similarities to the language of the synoptic Gospels under consideration in this study.]

Concerning Matthias' role–and this study's occasional reference to him

Matthias, a personage of importance in Jesus' life, who became the twelfth disciple replacing Judas Iscariot after the crucifixion, though not emphasized in this study, was apparently a major contributor to the Gospel record, ***and the only witness among the disciples at the Caiaphas hearing, judgment by Pilate, crucifixion, and entombment.***

Matthias' choice as a replacement of Judas Iscariot is documented in the New Testament (Acts I:20–I:26).

The relevant passage describing the moment reads:

> [Simon said] "We must choose someone who has been with us the whole time that the lord Jesus was traveling around with us, someone who was with us from the time when John was baptizing until the day when he was taken up from us—and he can act as witness to

his resurrection..." then they [voted]...and Matthias was listed as one of the twelve disciples [also called "apostles" after Jesus' death].

Matthias' role in creating the "new testament" is explicit. Simon says as much, with the words, "He can act as witness ..."

Based on further documentation, one may infer he was expected to record the disciples' recollections of Jesus' teaching and life. As the group's scribe, he would take down their "witnessed" testament.

(Note: Fictionalized in this author's historical novel, *The Matthias Scroll,* Matthias eventually sets about writing his own private scroll, determined to faithfully preserve Jesus' memory, recording the events as they actually happened.)

More Footprints Leading to Matthias' Historical Identity

In John 13:23, at the "Last Supper," Simon asks "the disciple Jesus loved" to inquire of Jesus who he meant would betray him.

Sitting at his side during the dinner, this mystery disciple's relationship with Jesus is such that he is presumed by Simon to know more about Jesus' preoccupation with the betrayal and impending arrest than any of the others.

After Jesus' arrest, when he is taken to the fateful hearing before Caiaphas, Simon is excluded, but "the disciple" is permitted to enter. Only when "the disciple" intercedes with a formal request, based on knowing Caiaphas personally (John 18:15–16), is Simon permitted to even enter the gated exterior courtyard. The relevant passage indicates the individual's administrative stature, plainly a man with authority, such as that of Matthias, purportedly a Sanhedrin scribe.

Simon-Peter and another disciple followed Jesus to Caiaphas' house (the hearing chamber). Since the disciple was known to the high priest (he) went with Jesus inside, but Simon was standing outside the door (courtyard gate). So the disciple, being known to the

> high priest, went out, spoke to the woman watching the
> gate, and brought Simon in (to the courtyard).

There, a fire had been lit and Simon was able to stay warm, along with the "servants and guards."

Several significant conclusions concerning the identity of "the disciple" emerge in this Gospel setting. First, he remained at Jesus' side, just as he had several hours earlier at the Last Supper. Therefore, we may infer it was the same person. Furthermore, having the stature of a scribe, he enabled Simon to enter the gated courtyard of the high priest. Of undeniable importance, the so-called disciple has enough political weight to be included at the hearing to witness the proceedings.

No other member of Jesus' circle is present as the interrogation begins—and plainly, only that individual could later provide any information about what occurred.

Recognizing his scribal status, one may logically infer that whatever record the Gospels make pertaining to Jesus' appearance before Caiaphas is drawn from the account subsequently offered by "the disciple"– arguably Matthias–and revised in Simon's version.

Not only was Matthias the single member of Jesus' entourage to witness the hearing before Caiaphas, but he, alone among the group, saw the grotesque mockery and derision at Pontius Pilate's Praetorium and Gabbatha scene of judgment.

Therefore, his detailed account would again constitute the only record of the event.

Two more chronicled appearances place him at the scene of the crucifixion and at the "empty tomb," with both accounts concealing the actual history beneath a heavy theological gloss.

As the only witness among Jesus' companions at the Caiaphas hearing, the judgment by Pilate, and the crucifixion, one may conclude that Matthias, having the skills of a scribe, could render a historical account of what actually occurred.

Why was his name expunged from the Gospels?

The evidence indicates he refused to exalt a glorified, supra-human Jesus.

As common sense suggests, whatever occurred to terminate Matthias' function as the group's scribe must have been tantamount to an emotional rupture. Almost certainly, the rift would have been accompanied by anger and, quite probably, mutual recrimination.

This author's surmise that Matthias had been Jesus' friend suggests he well-knew and rejected the messianic enhancement by Simon. More spiritual perjury than a simple act of exaggeration, Simon's postmortem exaltation of Jesus exhibited the very same reverence which ultimately enabled Antipas to charge him with sedition. On the road to Jerusalem for that fateful Passover, he had warned Simon to stop proclaiming him God's chosen king, or he would be killed. After his death, Matthias would not have helped spawn that twisted memory of who he was, a glorified image which Jesus had tried desperately to dispel.

In the Gospels, it is worth noting that the Greek for "disciple," *mathetes*, may indicate lack of belief in a teacher. In Acts 19:1, the term is applied to those who were ignorant of the holy spirit. Based on the Greek usage, one may conjecture that the Last Supper reference to "the disciple" originally relied on a finely drawn, disparaging vernacular.

Finally, the reader will find a brief discussion in Appendix C. of the post-Crucifixion Parable of the Wedding Banquet (Matthew 22:11-14). According to the text, the wedding of "the king's son" is "crashed" by a guest whom the king recognizes as an interloper, conspicuously not wearing the proper wedding garment (of belief in Jesus as the son of God). As he is thrown out, the king declares, "many are called, but few are chosen." The only disciple "called"–that is, invited, was Matthias, by Simon, to fill the place of Judas Iscariot. The others were "chosen" by Jesus when he was alive. Therefore, the parable's lesson is: If you are like Matthias, and do not have faith Jesus is God's son, you will be excluded from God's Kingdom when his rule as the groom on earth begins.

[Therefore, the one expelled (from Jesus' wedding to those who are saved through their faith in him) is Matthias—for not accepting his divine lineage.]

PART TWO

JESUS' BIOGRAPHY

DISCUSSION AND ANALYSIS, ILLUMINATING THE HISTORICAL SEQUENCE AND BIOGRAPHICAL IMPORTANCE OF CRITICAL GOSPEL PASSAGES

Discussions of the Gospel Content

1. Picking grain on Shabbat
2. Hand-washing episode: insult and contempt
3. Kfar Nahum episode
4. The holy spirit, the son of man, and sons of God
5. The Cana wedding
6. The adulteress woman
7. "Temptation" on the Jerusalem Temple mount
8. Jesus' baptism by John
9. Don't think I wish to abolish Torah
10. A paralyzed man lowered through the roof
11. Parables' biographical context
12. Jesus' eulogy for John
13. Jesus becomes a fugitive from Antipas (analysis of the "miracles": feeding the multitude loaves of bread and fish; walking on water; calming rough waves)
14. Simon, who do you say I am?
15. Jesus' final Passover

Including:

    a.   advance arrangements for the ceremonial meal

    b.   entry into Jerusalem

    c.   the meal ("last supper")

    d.   Judas' betrayal

    e.   arrest

    f.   hearing before Caiaphas

    g.   judgment before Pontius Pilate

    h.   crucifixion

    i.   entombment, disappearance

    j.   reconstructing what actually happened

    k.   who was Joseph of Arimathea?

16. Concluding thoughts

Picking grain on Shabbat

Mark 2:23-2:28; Matthew 12:1-8; Luke 6:1-5

At what exact point that spring-summer of 31CE Pietists began following Jesus to ascertain his teaching agenda is uncertain. Their investigative attitude, described in Mark 2:23-2:28 (also recorded in Matthew 12:1-8 and Luke 6:1-5), seems to first become apparent when they observe him and the disciples picking grain on the Shabbat. Here is the relevant passage (selectively combining the different Gospel texts):

> "One Shabbat he was going through the grain fields and as they made their way his disciples began to pluck ears of grain. And the Pietists said to him, 'Why are you doing what is unlawful on the Shabbat?' And he said to them, 'Have you never read what David did when he was in need and was hungry–he and those who were with him, how he entered the House of God when Abiathar was High Priest and ate the Bread of the Presence, which it is not lawful for any but the priests to eat, and also gave it to those who were with him?...I

tell you something greater than the Temple is here...for
the Son of Man is lord of the Sabbath.'"

Supposedly on a higher plane than David, who received the priest's
bread from "God's House" (a dwelling used by priests in the village
of Nob, before the Jerusalem Temple was built; ISamuel 21:5-6) the
Gospel portrays Jesus as not only having the prerogative to harvest
grain on the Shabbat, but as one divinely ordained to do so. As the text
states, "something greater than the Temple is here...for the Son of Man
is lord of the Sabbath."

To discern what truly occurred, it is useful to be familiar with the
Hebrew law concerning food-gathering by the poor. Based on the Torah
(Leviticus 19:9), God told Moses to command the People:

"When you gather the harvest of the land, you are not to harvest
to the very end (edge or corner) of the field. You are not to gather the
gleanings of the harvest...you must leave them for the poor and the
stranger..."

Furthermore, according to Deuteronomy 24:19, sheaves missed or
left standing were not to be harvested, but considered "forgotten" and
belonged to the poor. Rabbinic law emphasizes these injunctions in the
Talmud's tractate, Peah.

According to the Gospel passage, Jesus was in a grain field within
earshot of Pietists, presumably watching him from the adjacent road.
His disciples were therefore picking grain at the edge or corner of the
harvested area, as permitted the poor by Torah law.

On what basis, then, would the Pietists have protested he was
violating the commandment to keep the Shabbat?

Presumably, they were implying he and his group did not match
their idea of "the poor." In fact, if this were true, they were stealing from
the poor—by taking the grain left for those in need—and violating the
Shabbat as well. Jesus knew better. The rabbis, in their later Talmudic
exposition of these possibilities, decided a person who was not poor,
but was hungry at the time, could take the unharvested grain without
making restitution, explaining (Peah 5:4): "Because at that time (of
eating the grain) such a hungry person was, in effect, a poor man."

As for picking grain on the Shabbat, that too was no violation since the hungry were permitted to do so. In fact, the rabbis instructed (Peah 8:7), a larger donation of food to the poor was required on Shabbat, as long as there was no stacking or storage labor.

Replying to the suspicious Pietists who doubted their claim to being poor or hungry, Jesus gives expression to what would become Talmudic wisdom, saying, "The Shabbat is made for man—not man for the Shabbat." If his adversaries recognized the saying as a proverb of their own sages (Yoma 85b), his disciples did not. Believing the words revealed Jesus' divine authority over Torah law, they eventually preserved and recorded the episode as further evidence Jesus' words and acts had authority over Torah.

Regarding Jesus' supposedly comparing himself to King David, who is not being depicted as taking grain from a field, but, instead priests' bread from the Temple, the purpose is plainly to exalt Jesus. Further, his pronouncement "The Son of Man is lord of the Sabbath," is to publicize his messiahship to proselytes seeking some liturgical disclosure of his divine identity. The exalting comparison is so discordant as simply not to survive even minimal scrutiny, and should be set aside as having no shred of historic credibility.

The hand-washing episode: insult and contempt

Matthew 15:1-15:20; Mark 7:1-7:23

(Note: While this segment is concerned mainly with Jesus' adversaries, there were many mainstream Jews who observed household and personal purity laws. Unlike the Pietists, who are derided for religious exhibitionism by moderate Pharisees in the Talmud, others are not. See Talmud tractate Sotah 22b, delineating the "seven types of Pharisees" with mention of the "foolish Pietists," who are "hypocrites" and "ape the true Pharisees," exhibiting their supposed righteousness for all to see. Although redacted later, the Talmudic source preserves a perspective contemporaneous with Jesus).

According to the Galilean Pietists, God's Kingdom would commence only if Jewish purity standards met specific conditions matching the Jerusalem Temple protocol, conditions spelled out by the prophet Zechariah visa vie preparation for the Day of God–four centuries earlier.

In the scene depicted in Mark 7, wherein Jesus is criticized for not teaching his dinner companions to wash their hands before eating, the issue is his commitment to conditions of purity they have decreed necessary for God's Kingdom to commence.

Based on the viewpoint of the Pietists, he was thus showing indifference to the "household-as-Temple" concept–and disdain for their own group's leaders, typically rabbis, in their assumed role as a virtual priesthood.

The relevant passage reads (Mark 7:1-7:23):

> "Now (his Pietist adversaries)...noticed that some of his disciples were eating with defiled hands, that is, without washing them. For the Pharisees and all the Jews do not eat unless they wash their hands to the fist. And they do not eat anything from the market unless they totally wash it (or, 'unless they purify themselves')...(And their tradition is also to) wash cups, pots and bronze kettles. So (the Pietists) asked him, 'Why do your disciples not follow the tradition...but eat with defiled hands?'"

Jesus denounces the Pietists as hypocrites

Jesus replied: "Having abandoned the commandment of God, you are holding to the commandment of men," adding, "and you have set aside the commandment of God in order to keep your own traditions."

Noteworthy, in his reaction to their criticism is the deference he pays actual Torah law. What irritates him is not the Pietist habit of washing their hands before eating (something he probably did himself as a matter of hygiene, given they do not criticize his own deficiency in this regard). Instead, it is their sanctifying hand-washing, raising it to the level of a Torah commandment which rouses his indignation.

Because the stigma "am ha-aretz" (ignorant locals, see Part One, above) colored the image of Galilean peasants, unobservant of tithing requirements, the criticism directed at his companions implied they were Covenantal outcasts. Ignorance of Torah and the commandments was, in this milieu, considered a sign of lineage doubt—with possible ancestral sin staining an individual's Hebrew origins. The disciples' supposed ignorance of Torah law reflected by their indifference to hand-washing was, therefore, deemed a "symptom" of being a doubtful or lineage-defiled Hebrew.

But, as we see, Jesus turned tables on the critics of his disciples, focusing on their hypocrisy.

He tells them (selectively combining Matthew 15:5-6 and Mark 7:9-7:13 for clarity):

> "God commanded, 'Honor your father and your mother...' but you say, one who says to his father or mother, 'Whatever you would have received as support from me, I am giving (as a sacrifice/donation/tithe) to God.' (Therefore, an individual who follows this rule is) not permitted to do anything for his father or mother. And nullifying the word of God through your tradition, you pass it on (as if it is a commandment)."

Jesus, in responding to the Pietists' perceived hypocrisy (their having observed the tithing laws at the expense of their parents) has accused them of breaking one of the Ten Commandments (Honor your father and mother...) in order to sanctify a commandment they considered more important. As Jesus certainly was aware, breaking any Torah law, much less one of the most significant, in order to keep another, was strictly prohibited by rabbinic consensus.

Furthermore, he knew the Pietist edict was only another of their attempts to make themselves seem as holy as the Temple priesthood.

From a legal standpoint, there were two different issues: one, was whether handling food to be tithed required washed hands. It did. Food destined as a donation to the Temple could not be contaminated. However, on the occasion of the recriminatory exchange with the Pietists, there was another question: Was eating in a region outside the precincts of Jerusalem meant to be sanctified by the same laws of purity applicable to the Temple or foods being donated to it?

If the answer was in the affirmative, the food on the table of every Judean house had to be ritually supervised for purity. Commanded in that case, would be the hand-washing of participants prior to eating the meal. On the contrary, however, Torah law explicitly stated it was permissible to eat in an unclean state outside of Jerusalem (Deuteronomy 12:15).

Having called them hypocrites for changing Torah law to suit their pseudo-priestly charade, Jesus is not done. Recognizing they would exalt themselves over his group as if they were arbiters of God's will, judging the Covenantal legitimacy of his disciples, he struck back verbally.

To emphasize his resentment of their arrogance, Jesus says:

"There is no food which goes into a person that causes defilement –but the things that come out are what defile…(further explaining) since food does not enter the heart–but enters the stomach and goes into the sewer where all food is cleansed."

Telling from the text of Matthew 15:12 (wherein the disciples notice the Pietists are offended by his words) they grasped Jesus' insult: Just as food became feces, their words (which came out of the Pietists' mouths) were "a lot of crap."

Quite likely showing the audacity of a young man whose remarks had yet to be tempered by the habit of restraint, Jesus had made an indelible impression. About a year later, when he took the opportunity to chastise them for adultery, they would regard him as a hateful presence in their communities, leading to his banishment from the lakeside villages of Chorazin, Beit Zaida and Kfar Nahum.

[Note: It is the author's assertion that Jesus' rebuke of the three villages was his response to being banned from entering their districts (Matthew 11:21) which is historically followed by the "Sending out of the twelve disciples" (Matthew 9:37 and parallels), as he retreated from their midst.]

As the hand-washing episode continues, more of Jesus' actual words:

Matthew 15:11 quotes Jesus as saying: "It is not what goes into the mouth which defiles a man, but what comes out of his mouth" (followed by a list of transgressions in Matthew 15:19, such as "evil thoughts, murder, adultery, false witness, slander" all taken directly from the Torah. Matthew 15:20 concludes: "These are what defile a man, but to eat with unwashed hands does not defile a man."

Christianizing his words, the Gospel of Mark (7:15 and 7:19) alters Jesus comment:

"'There is nothing outside a man which by going into him can defile him...' thus he declared all foods clean." (The Greek may also be translated, "Thus all foods are cleansed.")

Yet, according to the passage, Jesus never says it is all right to eat "non-foods"–defined as such in Leviticus 11, most notably pork, or shell fish. Nor does he advocate eating meat cooked in dairy products, or the meat of animals cruelly slaughtered, or containing blood.

Why not? Is it possible he was nullifying the Torah's dietary laws with his own in the same breath he accused the Pietists of substituting their own laws for those of the Torah? And without even spelling out the details?

In fact, his own followers did not believe he had totally dispensed with the Torah's dietary laws. For after he died, there was a decree to pagan proselytes that they must not eat blood or the meat of strangled animals, though Jesus is never quoted as explicitly favoring these Torah commandments (Acts 21:25).

Some years after his death, when Jesus' followers expanded their evangelist efforts into areas where the normal diet was swine and seafood among other things, the question again arose. Did one from such a pagan background have to observe the dietary laws? Inasmuch as he had taught them "all food was clean/or cleansed" on the way to the sewer, they had to wonder whether that meant all life-forms were food. (As noted above, according to the Torah, the prohibited animal kinds were simply not food.)

Nonetheless, with the burden of ritual obligations threatening to deprive pagans of their daily fare, and thereby impeding conversions, Simon and Paul reach their agreement to adjust Jewish law to the circumstances of the fledgling church. In Romans 14:14, Paul states, "...I speak for Jesus that nothing one eats is unclean in itself..."

Here we have direct evidence that, in fact, Jesus did not emphasize the subject. Otherwise, Paul would not have had to "speak for him."

Simon's vision in Acts 10:10-10:16;11:6 does, however, show that the doctrine annulling the Torah's dietary commandments represented a change never advocated by Jesus. Descending from heaven, a spread-out sheet contains "every animal and bird, and everything possible that could walk, crawl, or fly." Resisting the temptation to eat, Simon is told, "Eat...what God has made clean, you have no right to call profane."

In sum, one may conclude that Jesus had downplayed hand-washing before eating—not as a rejection of Torah law—but as an affirmation of its correct interpretation. In so doing, he rejected the Pietists' pseudo-priesthood which considered the purity of their Galilean homes to be like the Jerusalem Temple. But, as the evidence shows, he never taught his followers to eat animals improperly slaughtered—or those life forms the Torah called "non-foods."

In contradistinction to his teaching, Christianity and the church have adopted the hand-washing episode as a basis for abandoning Hebrew dietary laws. Indeed, if one adheres to the view that Jesus advocated eating all life forms, he would have been equally ready to dispense with most ritual commandments forming the theological and cultural criteria of a Jewish lifestyle. As a result, the church upon which the disciples and apostles were constructing the new religion of universal salvation, claimed guidance from a heavenly Jesus, not the one who had historically been a devout Jew.

Kfar Nahum "exorcism"

Mark 1:23-28//Luke 4:33-37

The episode known as the Kfar Nahum (Capernaum) exorcism, occurring in the village synagogue, was disastrous for Jesus. Various startling aspects of the Gospel passage, taken together with subsequent events, support this assertion.

According to the Gospel description of the Kfar Nahum exorcism, the "possessed" congregant in the scene recognizes Jesus and knows where he is from: "What have you to do with us, Jesus of Nazareth?

Have you come to destroy us?! I know who you are!" he declares. [In both Mark 1:24 and Luke 4:34 the text adds (I know who you are) "the holy one of God..." which is a Christianizing gloss.]

In response, Jesus says, "Be quiet. Come out of him," which according to the description happens with screams and convulsions (Mark). And, he falls to the floor, unharmed and freed of the possession (Luke).

If the man in Kfar Nahum was thought by the congregation to be possessed, the exorcism would likely have been regarded as an unpleasant distraction from the Shabbat service, best performed outside. Even conducted in their midst, the exorcism would likely have impressed many and been a minimal cause of controversy. But, if the worshippers witnessing the event thought the supposedly possessed congregant was normal–and Jesus was silencing him–the scene takes on a different meaning.

If that occurred, the roles were, in fact, reversed. The man declaring, "What have you to do with us, Jesus of Nazareth? Have you come to destroy us?! I know who you are!" would be voicing the suspicions of his fellow-congregants. Now Jesus would be the adversary of a devout Jew whose collapse and convulsions were due to an attack on his inner being, his Hebrew soul.

As startling as this scenario may seem, it is what happened. In Luke 4:23, a remark made by Jesus soon after, while experiencing rejection in the vicinity of his hometown Nazareth synagogue, recalls the Kfar Nahum exorcism which had apparently become the subject of rumor and gossip. "No doubt," Jesus tells those Nazareth congregants, "you will quote me the proverb, 'Physician heal yourself,' and say to me, 'We have heard all that happened in Kfar Nahum...'"

"Heal yourself," could not refer to a medical problem since Jesus had no physical malady. The words Jesus was using referred to a spiritual disorder, namely possession. In other words, Jesus knew that many of the Nazareth congregants considered him to be the one possessed and in need of an exorcism–not them.

In ascribing their antagonistic attitude to "what happened in Kfar Nahum," he leaves no doubt that the exorcism there was its cause.

Gossip that Jesus' exorcisms were inspired by an evil agenda, thus laid the foundation for the suspicion he was sent by the satanic deity, Beelzebul. ("The prince of devils" is a description of Beelzebul used against Jesus in Mark 3:22.)

To be sure, the Gospels portray Jesus as fully cognizant of the Pietists' accusation—that he had "silenced" a devout Jew. Such is the clear meaning of Jesus' denial that he had ever done such a thing. To wit, his famed remarks (Matthew 12:25-37//Mark 3:23-30//Luke 11:17-23): "If Satan casts out satan (that is, does an exorcism) how will his kingdom (which they suspect Jesus of engendering) exist?" In other words, if Jesus had done the Kfar Nahum exorcism on a normal Jew he could not logically have been an agent of satan. Instead, he would wish the enraged congregant to remain possessed. Therefore, whether the man did or did not have a demon was not indicative of Jesus' supposed evil identity. Still, the rumor became reality in the minds of the Pietists, quite probably offended that Jesus presumed to "heal" one of their own— as if he had tried to eradicate the man's Pietist persona.

Analysis of the Kfar Nahum passage

That the man (and not a demon, as described) apparently recognized Jesus to be from Nazareth is highly plausible, given the nexus of small communities extending from Nazareth to the lakeside. Gossip and rumor were the journalism of the day and Jesus' notoriety plainly found a receptive audience as word spread.

The next phrase, found in both Mark 1:24 and Luke 4:34 (I know who you are) "the holy one of God..." is a Christianizing gloss which also serves as an editorial patch meant to create a thematic seam with the parallel words of demons in the adjacent Lukan passage, declaring, "You are the son of God" (Luke 4:41).

Did the Kfar Nahum man actually say, "You have come to destroy us"? (Or, having the same syntax, as a question, "Have you come to destroy us?")

Whether a question or an assertion, they were assuredly the words the man uttered. The fact is, there is no other passage in the Gospels wherein demons recognize Jesus' intent to destroy them. Even in the story of the Gerasene exorcism (Mark 5:1-5:13 and //'s), the demons ask only whether Jesus intends to "torment" them. Therefore, unglossed by editorial enhancement, the man's terrified elocution is authentic.

In the Gospels' subsequent depictions (Luke 4:41//Mark 1:34) that Jesus silenced demons to prevent them from exposing his messianic identity (before God's schedule), such admonitions are in sharp stylistic contrast to the exorcism at Kfar Nahum. There, no explicit agenda of secrecy occurs–though Pietists would later regard it as an effort to prevent the man from exposing his evil identity.

In sum, based on these various elements, the following conclusion may be drawn: The man in the Kfar Nahum synagogue recognized Jesus and thought, according to the rumors he had heard, that Jesus was evil, even an emissary of Beelzebul. When he said so, ranting and raving his accusation out of terror, Jesus took him for one possessed and pronounced the exorcism formulation, "Come out of him," whereupon the man collapsed. To those who witnessed the scene, fellow congregants who believed the one on the ground was a devout and normal man, his falling down like that seemed proof of what he had alleged. He had recognized Jesus, attempted to reveal his evil identity, and Jesus had silenced him by causing him to go into convulsions.

The holy spirit, the son-of-man, and sons of God
Mark 3:28-3:29; Matthew 12:32; Luke 12:10

When he departed Kfar Nahum, after the ill-conceived "exorcism," and arrived in Nazareth, Jesus was soon confronted by Pietists. Having heard about the "false exorcism," they warned others he was covenanted with Satan (aka "Beelzebul"). Especially after his scathing insults directed at their religious hypocrisy (see hand-washing confrontation above), the Pietists had a visceral aversion to Jesus and denounced him as possibly evil. To them, his healings of chronic, sometimes life-long afflictions, such as paralysis and atrophied limbs, or dropsy, were tantamount to claims of divine power. Gossip that he did so in synagogues on Shabbat and had even extended his "forgiveness" to a leper, added to their suspicion he was playing the messiah (Mark 1:40-45).

They characterized his healing, so similar to their own, with a compassionate touch, kind words, a promise of hope and a blessing–as originating from the spirit of Satan. Kfar Nahum was etched in their minds, a turning point representing the first concrete act on Jesus' part which they could label evil.

In response to their Beelzebul-satan accusation, Jesus pronounced what may stand as his most important expression of an authentic, personal theology. As such, it warrants considerable attention.

In Mark 3:28-3:29, Jesus reportedly says:

"All sins will be forgiven the sons-of-men and whatever blasphemies they utter, but whoever blasphemes against the holy spirit never has forgiveness but is guilty of eternal sin..."

In Matthew 12:32 and Luke 12:10, the parallel passage reads:

"Whoever says a word against the Son-of-Man (capitalized here to indicate its use as a transcendental title), will be forgiven, but whoever speaks against the holy spirit will not be forgiven."

In the latter text, Matthew 12:32//Luke 12:10–according to Christian dogma–Jesus refers to himself as the "Son-of-Man," presumably a divine manifestation of God, taking the form of a human being. Christianity's "human" Jesus, having earthly travails, is thus realistically accepting the intolerance directed at him. However–his divine origin, an emanation of God's Spirit (the holy spirit), must not be demeaned (that is called evil) or eternal punishment may result.

How may we be certain the Son-of-Man named in Matthew 12:32// Luke 12:10 has presumed divine attributes? The usage in Matthew 24:30, Mark 13:26 and Luke 21:27 is explicit. Those texts (with minor variation) state: "(on the Day of Judgment) they will see the Son of Man coming on the clouds of heaven with power and great glory...and he will send out the angels..."

Shortly, we shall examine the character biblically known as the "Son-of-Man," focusing on Jesus' possible self-identification with him. For now, it is sufficient to understand that, according to Matthew 12:32 and Luke 12:10, Jesus supposedly adopted it as a messianic title.

Mark, however, has a revealing alteration to this text. Note that 3:28-3:29 makes no mention of the Son of Man, but records Jesus' words as: "all sins will be forgiven the *sons of men...*" (my italics). Both passages refer to insulting the holy spirit as a grave sin, indicating they record the same declaration–but that is all they have in common.

As we proceed, one plain fact should be kept in mind: Jesus did not say both things. That is, he did not speak of the sins of the "sons of men" (Mark 3:28) as well as "Whoever says a word against the Son of Man..." (referring to himself, Matthew 12:32).

Perhaps the first step in retrieving Jesus' actual words is to recognize the implication of the term "sons of men." Jesus is talking about the sins of those who slandered him by calling him evil. If he meant ordinary people (Pietists, others) as he did, one can infer that the term, a plural, could also be used as a singular: "son of man."

Logically if "sons of men" simply meant more than one ordinary person, a "son of man" was just an individual–not a divine figure to come on clouds at the End of Days.

If we substitute the pedestrian usage for the divine Son of Man, we have the following:

(Mark 3:28) **"All sins will be forgiven the sons of men and whatever blasphemies they utter**

(now inserting Matthew 12:32, changing divine Son of Man to an ordinary person, singular:) **against this son of man.**

And, putting these together: **"all sins will be forgiven the sons of men and whatever blasphemies they utter against this son of man**

And, finishing the statement without any revision:

But whoever blasphemes against the holy spirit has no forgiveness, and they will not be forgiven in this age or the age to come."

Thus, the complete, authentic rendering of Jesus' words is:

"All sins will be forgiven the sons of men and whatever blasphemies they utter against this son of man. But whoever blasphemes against the holy spirit has no forgiveness, and they will not be forgiven in this age or the age to come."

Further evidence does exist that 1. the "divine" Son of Man nomenclature was never spoken by Jesus, and 2. that his self-identification as such, is false.

In the Biblical "Book of Daniel" (7:13), a divine figure "coming on the clouds of heaven" has "glory and kingship" and "an eternal sovereignty which shall never pass away..."

Having been written approximately a century-and-a-half before Jesus, with identical language and imagery, we may be confident this was the source of the Gospel usage.

Who is the divine figure coming on clouds? Daniel's answer is: "He was one *like* a son of man..."

The wording "like a son of man" indicates he looked human. This is not the same as saying he was the Son of Man. Therefore, in the Book of Daniel the son of man is a way of saying, "human."

Supporting this assertion, the text of Daniel 8:17 has the angel Gabriel address Daniel (!), saying, "son of man, understand (your vision this way)..." phrasing which leaves no doubt that the title, as Christianized in Matthew 12:32, is an aggrandizement. The attempt to make Jesus, who refers to himself as an ordinary human being (son of man) seem divine, should be set aside.

Any remaining sentiment attaching a supposed divine identity to the "Son of Man" evaporates when measured against an even earlier source of the same imagery and form of address, found in the book of the prophet Ezekiel.

The prophet's vision describes "a being that looked like a man" seated on a heavenly throne, speaking to him. The divine figure addresses the prophet, saying, "son of man, I am sending you to the Israelites..." (2:3).

(In the book of Ezekiel, this form of address occurs repeatedly.)

Lastly, I should point out that the Hebrew translation of "son of man" is "ben-adam," or in Aramaic, "bar-enosh," which simply means "son of Adam." As a descendant ("son") of Adam, the individual was simply a person.

The holy spirit

As the reader may be aware, the term is today a cornerstone of Christian dogma, theologically embraced as one of the three manifestations of God: "The Father, the Son, and the Holy Spirit."

Almost certainly, if one were to ask a knowledgeable Jewish individual, including scholars and rabbis about the "holy spirit," most would say it is part of the Christian "Trinity."

In fact, its origins are Hebrew and its spiritual role in the Torah is one of pervasive theological importance. In a word, had the Hebrew religion not engendered belief in the "holy spirit," nobody would have known what Jesus was talking about when he referred to it.

What exactly was the "holy spirit" and when did it originate as an idea?

In the earliest periods portrayed in Genesis, it is referred to as "the spirit/the spirit of Adonai."

A closer look

The first occurrence of the "spirit" is found in the opening lines of the Book of Genesis, stating, "God's Spirit hovered over the waters." And, we behold the awesome "birth" of the world from an unformed state. Created, perhaps, from God's own essence (since nothing else except God existed), matter was transformed by the Divine Spirit from a chaotic state, to differentiation and order.

The Hebrew is revealing. God's "Spirit" is the general English translation of "ruach"–a synonym for "wind." An alternate translation results in: "God's wind hovered over the waters..."

When Adam is created (Genesis 2:7), a direct correlation between air and God is again described: "Then the Lord...breathed into (Adam's) nostrils the breath of life and man became a living soul."

In this passage, the word for "breathe" and the word for "soul" are the same, having the Hebrew root n-sh-m. Based on the usage, it is not a stretch to conclude that man's soul is here represented as closely related to the "breath"–or "Spirit" of God. Furthermore the Spirit of God is progenitive–having created the world, and the first humans.

Familiar with these texts, first century Christians would have comfortably associated the baptism/immersion as replicating the primordial creation, inasmuch as they believed Jesus was ushering in God's Kingdom. For the baptized individual to receive God's Spirit (that is, the Divine breath) upon surfacing, and to be "re-born," he had only to be included as a member of the faithful Christian community.

Furthermore, such progeny of God's breath would, as the Torah states, be "in the likeness of God's image" (Genesis 1:27). What exactly did "being created in God's image" entail? One of the more obscure passages of Genesis (chapter 6) describes divine sonship. It reads: "The sons of God saw the daughters of men...and took them as wives..."

The same text continues: "...the Lord said, My Spirit ('ruach,' as hovered over the waters) shall not abide in man forever, since he too is flesh (like the daughters of men)" and therefore humans would live a finite number of years (as the Spirit/breath of the Creator was removed).

As seemingly bizarre as this passage is, we may extract from it something about "the likeness" of God. Originally God's breath had made humans immortal—"like" God. Early on, however, the Divine Spirit was removed and the resulting humans were relegated to mortality.

Later, about 1250 BCE, Moses laments: "If only all God's People were prophets, and the Lord put His spirit upon them" (Numbers 11:29).

The exact use of the Hebrew term ("ruach ha-kodesh"=holy spirit) first becomes explicit about a millennium before Jesus, in the period of the Hebrew monarchy (Saul, David, and Solomon), a discussion of which is beyond the parameters of these brief remarks.

It does repeatedly recur in sacred Hebrew texts, playing an important role in God's communication with the prophets (for example, Ezekiel and Joel) and in the Dead Sea writings ("Thanksgiving Hymns" and other sections).

In this light we may now ask what exactly was the role of the "holy spirit" as Jesus understood it, and what were its characteristics in the Gospels?

At the moment of his conception, the holy spirit appears in a procreative function. The announcement by an angel (known in Christian vernacular as "the Annunciation") of Mary's impending pregnancy is portrayed as an act of the holy spirit, since she "has no husband" (Luke 1:34-35). And, according to the passage, "the child will be called the son of God." (Matthew 1:18 is a parallel passage.)

Also in the Gospels, it is associated with the baptism. When Jesus is immersed by John, he emerges from under the water, and the holy spirit "descended upon him" (Luke 3:22). Matthew 3:16 and Mark 1:10 say only that "the spirit of God" or "the spirit" descended on him. All three quote a voice from heaven declaring, "[This is/thou art] my beloved son."

Therefore, we may deduce the holy spirit in the Gospels could turn an individual into a "son" of God. Though no Hebrew scripture ever attributed actual conception to the holy spirit, precedent was well-established that individuals touched by its presence, could be "sons of God." Jesus himself quotes Psalm 82:6 (in John 10:34) to make the same point.

Imbued with a belief in these "powers" of the holy spirit, assuredly drawn from earlier Hebrew scripture, Jesus would have encouraged his disciples to feel like legitimate members of the Jewish community, inheritors (sons) of the Covenant. His Torah-teaching, imbuing them with the holy spirit, reflected the established perception and practice of venerated rabbis of his era. Such teaching was an act tantamount to vitiating all doubt about their family tree, so that their newfound knowledge of Torah might make them "sons of God" (the title they would earn by study with him).

(Note: In Shaaray Kedusha, preserving the much-earlier tradition, the 16th century Kabbalist, Rabbi Hayim Vital states: "The holy spirit can be attained through Torah study.")

Therefore, beyond conjecture, Jesus believed the holy spirit flowed from his Torah teaching and could help them return from social and religious exile to their Covenantal home, restored as members of the Hebrew People.

Such was Jesus' reverence for the holy spirit, he stated that any personal insult toward him would not jeopardize the Pietists' Covenantal future—but sternly admonished them not to demean the holy spirit lest they risk any chance of "forgiveness." As he saw it, maligning him as satanic, though a sin (as it would be if directed toward any citizen) could be atoned. But an insult to the "holy spirit" was blasphemy—a sin against God (Matthew 12:22-12:32).

In sum, Jesus' believed the holy spirit enabled him, as it did other rabbis, to Covenantally restore those disciples who had tarnished ancestral lineages or personally strayed from the path of Torah. Unlike the Pietists, he believed even those completely unobservant and ignorant of Jewish culture, who responded to Torah "with ears to hear" thereby purified their family tree and made themselves worthy of rejoining the Hebrew community.

The Cana wedding

John 2:1-2:12

My reconstruction of the wedding at Cana (John 2:1-2:12) illuminates what actually occurred. As presented in the Gospel of John, the scenario is strictly for the faithful Christian. The style of the passage is "midrashic," a lesson-legend with a historical core.

The main elements of the wedding party as they appear in the Gospel of John:

1. His disciples accompany him to the wedding (2:2).
2. Jesus' mother says, "They have no wine."
3. Jesus says to her, "What is that to me and you, woman? My hour has not come yet."
4. (Then) his mother says to the servants, "Do whatever he tells you."
5. (To the servants) he next says, "Fill the jars with water..."– referring to spigotted hand-washing vessels near the door–and he performs the miracle, turning the water to wine (2:7-2:9).
6. The steward, receiving the wine from the servants, unaware of the "miracle," tells the groom, "Everyone serves the good wine first and then the inferior wine after the guests have become drunk (had plenty to drink). But you have kept the best wine until now."
7. (This was the first of the signs...and his disciples believed in him)... "After this he went down to Kfar Nahum with his mother and his brothers (and the disciples) but they stayed there only a few days" (2:12).

Analysis and reconstruction:

Jesus' response to his mother's statement that they have no wine: "What is that to you and to me, woman? My hour has not come yet," is, in tone, an irritable if not angry rejoinder. Had he said, "Mother, don't be concerned," the moment between them would have been respectful and even affectionate.

Several possible explanations exist: 1. This is one among several passages showing that his relationship to his biological family was not equal to his bond with devotees (a Christianizing interpretation). 2. He and his mother weren't getting along. 3. He was annoyed by Mary's implied criticism that he had come too late for the guests to care about his (hypothetical) gift of wine.

Certainly, Jesus' reactions to his family are distant and cool throughout the Gospels. (Note: Although I believe James was a deeply devoted sibling, the evidence of his interaction with Jesus is limited and circumstantial.)

The second and third alternatives—that Jesus and his mother were not getting along—taken together with his annoyance at her dismissive greeting, therefore seems likely. His mother's anxiety, reflected in the Nazareth-synagogue scene (Mark 3:31-3:35) reveals the family concern that he was acting "crazy." Criticized for "playing the prophet," and making a public display of what they considered ridiculous antics, Jesus had expressed his irritation, rebuffing them.

The second part of his response, "My hour has not come yet" is informative. We know this was not referring to his "hour" to help out with the depleted wine supply. Theologically, it has an unmistakeable ring of a future revelation that he is the messiah. (That is, "My time to reveal myself as the messiah has not come yet," which is plainly irrelevant to a non-messianic context.)

Far more credible is her initial reference to wine because, hypothetically, she observed the wineskin he had brought as a gift. Mary, I propose, was actually castigating his tardy arrival, indicating his wine was "too little, too late." Then, as a logical reaction to Mary's criticism that they were already out of wine, he might well reply: "What's it to you and me, woman. It's not my wedding."

According to my reconstruction:

Shortly after his abrupt remarks to his mother, he instructs the servants to mix the wine he has brought as a gift into the hand-washing jars which are arrayed near the entrance.

His intention to use ritual washing vessels to dispense wine was in total disregard of the feelings of traditional guests at the party. More than that, it would have been an affront likely to cause their outspoken indignation.

Seeing the servants hesitate, Mary sought a quick resolution of the issue, lest Jesus once again become conspicuous. Therefore, she orders the servants to "Do whatever he tells you."

After pouring in the wine, the servant brings some to the steward, who tastes it and offers his compliments to the groom.

In the Gospel account (2:10) he says: "People generally serve the best wine first and keep the inferior sort til the guests have become drunk (had plenty to drink); but you have kept the best wine until now."

In fact, not uncommon in such first century Judean celebratory circumstances, when the wine supply was diminished, increasing amounts of water were added to it. Therefore, early on, the party would have been drinking (perhaps) a fifty-fifty mixture of wine and water (or even a higher percentage of wine), and later, a less tasty mixture with increasing amounts of water.

If some of the guests, or the wine steward himself, commented on the rich mixture, their surprise could well have been (variously): "People generally serve the strongest wine first and water it down later, but we have the strongest wine last," or, if offered as a compliment to the groom, "Common people save the cheap wine until everyone is drunk but you have saved the best until now!"

Significantly, my analysis of the Gospel account further reveals the water-to-wine "miracle" was a postmortem alteration intended to establish Jesus as a holier version of the high priest in Jerusalem. The Hebrew festival of Sukkot had a central ritual in which water was poured simultaneously with wine on the Temple altar. The water-libation ceremony, as it was called, enacted the fall seasonal miracle when rainfall, a blessing from God, nurtured the vineyards, miraculously turning to wine.

Every guest at the Cana party who believed Jesus was "playing the miracle-worker" now had a joke at his expense. Though he was not mixing the wine and water to mimic the Sukkot ceremony, the sarcastic interpretation was inevitable. "Look at him now–turning water to wine like the high priest!" (This sarcasm was transformed by the Gospel into reverence and wonder, recording it as "the first of the signs.")

Judging from what followed, Mary, the disciples who were there, and his supposed own half-brothers (the sons of Joseph being actual cousins if Joseph was not Jesus' father), were embarrassed.

What did Mary say to Jesus when guests began taking notice? Recreating her words (based on his response upon arriving, "it's not my wedding") I propose she then insisted, "If you keep acting like this, nobody will marry you!" Evidence for her hypothetical remark are the words he spoke which are not repeated in the Gospel version, but seem likely to have echoed the same sentiment as "My hour has not come yet." In the course of the wedding party, her comment, "if you keep acting like this, nobody will marry you" would very possibly have been met with the retort: "I'm not ready to get married." (This last line becomes the Gospel rendering, "My hour has not come yet.") Still, a question arises: In the midst of her discomfort at his perceived "antics," why should she have chosen to make Jesus' future marriage an issue? I submit there was a significant reason: If people regarded Jesus as genuinely mad, they would likely believe him to be a "shetuki," one who had no known father. (The popular saying was, "Shetuki is shetufi"–the one who cannot name his father acts like a crazy person.) Consequently, he would be ineligible to marry a woman of known Hebrew lineage, mixing the "certain with the doubtful" (prohibited by Jewish custom). Causing Mary further anguish, quite naturally, would be the resulting opinion that she had been guilty of adultery (in that his seemingly bizarre behavior indicated Joseph was not his father).

Aside from Mary's distress, I suggest the moment was also troubling to Jesus' siblings (setting aside the paternal doubt) and disciples. Here is the evidence they left without him: At the outset (John 2:2) we are told,

"Jesus and his disciples had also been invited." At the end of the scene, the passage states (2:12): "After this he went down to Kfar Nahum with his mother, and the brothers."

Here is the reconstruction:

1. Jesus and his disciples arrive at the Cana wedding party bringing wine as a gift.
2. The party has been underway for some time, and Jesus' mother greets him, saying: "They have no wine"–a criticism implying that his gift is "too little, too late."
3. Jesus, apparently aggravated by her tone, as well as still resenting her earlier effort at the Nazareth synagogue to stop him from "playing the prophet," replies: "What's it to me or you, woman. It's not my wedding."
4. Inside, he hands the wineskin to a servant and tells him to pour it into a spigotted vessel used for hand-washing. (To a Pietist or other strictly observant Jews, such vessels had achieved an aura of holiness, reflecting the belief all houses would need to be pure before God's Kingdom could commence.)
5. When the servant hesitates, Mary instructs him to "Do whatever he tells you."
6. After the wine-water mixture, now enriched, is taken to the steward, he tastes it and pays the groom a compliment: "People usually serve the strongest wine first and water it down later, but you have saved the best for last!"
7. Hypothetical: Guests joked, "Look what he has done now, playing the high priest, turning water to wine!"
8. Hypothetical: Comments were made, such as: "Shetuki is shetufi–crazy ones cannot say who their father is."
9. Dismayed, Mary tells Jesus: (words inferred from his next response):
   "If you keep acting like this, nobody will marry you."
10. Jesus replies: "I'm not ready to get married." (Echoing his earlier remark, "It's not my wedding" and "my hour has not yet come."

11. Hypothetical: Jesus becomes aware that he is not Joseph's son. (The subsequent events strongly suggest Mary's warning had "hit home." Saying he would never marry if he kept up his "antics," she had basically divulged the truth.

12. The disciples, perhaps unnerved by the apparent family squabble, depart.

13. Jesus along with his brothers (still called that, though, unlike them, he was unrelated to Joseph), left with Mary and went to Kfar Nahum. (Though the Gospels do not say as much, Kfar Nahum was probably the village where one or more of Joseph's sons lived.)

Recognizing the timeframe as the fall Sukkot pilgrimage festival (Feast of Booths), I suggest that from this text we may discern who among them intended to make the two-three day journey from Kfar Nahum to Jerusalem.

According to John 7:3, as the Feast of Booths drew near, Jesus' brothers said to him:

> "Why not leave this place (Kfar Nahum) and go to (Jerusalem) and let your disciples see the works you are doing. If a man wants to be known, he does not do things in secret. Since you are doing all this you should let the whole world see."

This remarkable comment by Joseph's sons, whom he had long-considered his brothers, is sarcasm. The Gospel text which immediately follows leaves no doubt: "Not even his brothers, in fact, had faith in him."

In what may be the Gospels' only description of an emotionally hurt Jesus, he tells his brothers: (7:7-7:8) "The world cannot hate you, but it does hate me." Of special importance, is his use of the word, "cannot." Assuredly there is a reason why they are "above" the possibility of being hated. Here, I think it is inescapable that he is referring to their pure Hebrew lineage, fixing their status as irreproachably free from the common contempt the society showed those with doubtful origins. In that he says this immediately after the Cana wedding party, I strongly suspect he had learned Joseph was not his father right about then.

(Note: The typical church interpretation of the word "brothers" is that they were devotees–and not members of his family. Probably because dogma requires Jesus have a "family-of-the-faithful," the role of Joseph's sons is largely muted. An even superficial analysis of the text exposes the fact the ones referred to in the Cana story were absolutely Joseph's sons.

First, it makes no sense to tell his followers, suddenly called "brothers" and not "disciples" that "they cannot hate you" when throughout the Gospels his students are reviled. Further, we all know the grotesque persecution suffered by the early Christians. Second, in expressing their sarcastic insult, "Go to Jerusalem and let your disciples see the works you are doing..."(John 7:2-7:6) the brothers hardly sound like a family-of-the-faithful.

But before setting out alone, finally making the decision to go to Jerusalem on Sukkot, Jesus has a troubling vision. It is one which conjecture suggests was directly related to finding out about his paternal origin.

The Adulterous Woman

John 8:1-8:11

The disastrous reality Jesus uncovers at Cana–that he was born to an unknown father–has ramifications beyond the limits it may place on his future marital options. The very faith he has so devoutly taught his disciples has been questioned by Pietists. If he has a possibly satanic paternal origin, he has to wonder whether his adversaries are right–that he has been misguiding his devoted followers with evil falsehoods– letting them believe in him–instead of God. If his actual father was a foreigner, perhaps an idolater–Jesus must ponder whether he could have been an unwitting emissary of beliefs he never intended to espouse. Of course, he had meant to exalt Torah's commandments–but what if the impression he gave was that they didn't matter? Or, that he could overrule the laws of Shabbat...and forgive sins, even the punishments from God causing afflictions like leprosy?

Staggered by self-doubt, quite assuredly before he departed for the Sukkot Feast of Booths, which he finally decided to attend, he had a vision. It is recorded in the Gospel of John 8:1-8:11 as "The Adulterous Woman."

This odd passage is clarified by Jesus learning he is not Joseph's son (at Cana) and that he is the progeny of Mary's adultery. Furthermore, there is an echo of the form of address Jesus uses in the Cana scene to his mother, "Woman..." (John 2:4) as compared to addressing the adulteress (John 8:10) "Woman..."

As a midrash explaining an actual historical event, Christianity had only one reason to include it at all. Something had happened that needed explaining. As a matter of record, women were rarely, if ever, caught committing adultery. Two eyewitnesses might see a woman flirting with a man—and enable a husband to demand a divorce, but not accuse her of actual fornication, with stoning the resulting punishment. John 8, therefore, is not what it seems. Almost certainly, Jesus' beautiful, poetic act of compassion and forgiveness evokes a highpoint of his spirituality. One of the most trying moments in his life, he looks at the sad visage before him, and says unequivocally that he does not condemn her—even though what she has done may condemn him. It is, in the opinion of this author, almost certainly his own mother. Mary, as a young girl of sixteen, soon to be married to a man in his forties, had a romantic interlude. Her pregnancy was proof of adultery—but only if Joseph brought charges, something he would never do against his own niece. Even the Gospel of Matthew hints this saying Joseph was "an honorable man" (Matthew 1:19). Violation of a betrothal, according to Jewish law, was adultery. And, Joseph, an uncle who had been married to Mary's deceased blood-aunt, never accused her, but raised Jesus until he was twelve. (The assertion that the "adulteress woman" is Jesus' mother, perhaps a reality he described to Matthias, is derived as a hypothesis clarified from the Cana wedding interpretation and further links to the episodes which follow. Because, however, it does not clarify other obscure Gospel text, it is not "tested" by the method of precipitous insight and must remain conjecture.)

Proceeding further with logical inferences, we should concentrate on the reality that his disciples had gone on without him. Choosing to remain alone, he says to his brothers (restored syntax 7:8-7:9) "Go to the festival yourselves. I am not going to this festival."

In 7:10 the text states he changed his mind and went to Jerusalem by himself.

Is there further evidence that Jesus' disciples had indeed set out and reached Jerusalem for the Sukkot festival, arriving there before him?

In John 1:36-1:45 the text mentions Jesus' (supposed) first encounter with John (the Baptist), as well as various disciples. Though the report of the disciples' presence occurs in an out-of-sequence scene in the vicinity of John's baptisms, it belongs with the Sukkot timeframe. (Note: It is a consistent kerygmatic intervention that places the baptism of Jesus, as well as John's witness to his chosen status, at the beginning of Jesus' ministry, leaving us to locate it correctly, which we shall do just below the next episode.)

"Temptation" on the Jerusalem Temple mount

Matthew 4:1-4:11; Mark 1:12-1:13; Luke 4:1-4:13

According to the Gospel account, Jesus having just been baptized by John, anointing him the "son of God," is taken by the devil up the Temple mount in Jerusalem (Matthew 4:5), who showed him "all the kingdoms" he would rule (Luke 4:5)—if he would throw himself over the edge of the precipice. Supposedly, by not being hurt, he would prove he was the son of God—and then the devil would give him the world. If this doesn't seem to make sense, there is a reason. The historical facts were among the most difficult to Christianize. As a result, the "story" is strained and illogical. Not only does it fail as a supernatural dramatization, but as a logical, coherent tale. Nonetheless, as a "midrash" (see Introduction and subsequent remarks on this literary genre popular in Jesus' era), the legend-lesson of the "temptation" conceals a historical core. For reasons which will become apparent, the Gospel version places the baptism of Jesus sequentially before the "temptation." Recognizing it occurred immediately afterwards illuminates the historical link connecting the episodes.

The disjointed description has as its central component that Jesus believes the devil has power to offer him sovereignty over the world. According to the text, he doesn't doubt the devil's words—but refuses to put God to the test (Mark 4:7). In Luke 4:8 Jesus refuses to jump because he's only "supposed to worship God."

In their bizarre exchange, the devil scoffs that as the "son of God" he should be immune to injury from such a horrendous fall. Jesus is tempted because if he takes the leap, the rocks below will turn to bread, and he is hungry. Of course, not only will he have bread to eat, but he will have proved he is God's son, and, thanks to the devil, can assume his reign.

If there is a "temptation," it is to set aside these passages as unworthy of analysis. However, quite to the contrary, the strained text is the very evidence there is something hidden—something which needed to be Christianized or it could be a threat to the image of Jesus as the messiah.

Clues and evidence

During the Sukkot (Feast of Booths) festival (just occurring, as established in the Cana discussion above), it was customary to reflect on the "yetzer ra" (evil inclination) and the "yetzer tov" (good inclination). Over centuries, the evil inclination eventually developed a poetic personification as "satan"—actually a Hebrew word meaning "tempter." Though the term morphed into a popular super-demon, it never became more than a marginal folk personality in Judaism. According to tradition, the inclination to evil, "yetzer ra"—when faced with temptation ("satan") could cause evil choices.

With this as the first century Jewish background, we must next consider what might have actually caused Jesus' encounter with "temptation."

Until the Cana wedding, he could confidently reject all the criticism by Pietists, neighbors, and family that he was acting like a crazy person.

His maligned exorcism on a healthy, normal Jew whom he supposedly caused to convulse on a synagogue floor (see Kfar Nahum, above), taken together with healing diseases of punishment –as though he could forgive sins, along with interpreting the Shabbat, as if he were its master–all were spurious accusations which he had dismissed as ignorant foolishness.

After Cana, that changed. (See Cana, above.)

If his father was unknown, and his mother was an adulteress, his teaching and healings were possibly sinful, just as the critics said. If he had been exalting himself as a great interpreter of Torah, twisting its passages to suit his image–even as one who could save others–that inclination would be "yetzer ra," an inclination to follow evil, yielding to the temptation (satan) to rule others.

For the first time, he doubted himself. The truths he espoused had possibly been distortions, and, now even more suspect, was the conviction that he was being guided by God's Spirit. Maybe it wasn't God–but, he feared, the inherited, deformed voice of his unknown father–contaminated further by an adulterous union–of which he was the progeny. Such were his doubts as he ascended the Temple mount on that Sukkot.

(Note: The Christianized location is a small mountain on the road between Jerusalem and Jericho. I see no reason to accept that site as anything more than doctrinal fantasy, a common occurrence in attributing Gospel episodes to suitable geographical candidates devoid of textual substantiation.)

Despairing that he had possibly diminished Torah to exalt himself, using it as a tool to promote his disciples' reverence–even permitting them to believe he was a voice of God–Jesus stood on the edge of the Temple's precipice, preferring to die rather than further mislead his followers. At this moment of great personal crisis, he decided against taking his life, instead resorting to the immersion by John to purify his lineage and atone his sins.

Though the Gospels suggest he continued his healings, objective scrutiny of all subsequent activity tells a different story. His "overruling" the Shabbat–or forgiving sin...whatever he had done or said to give the impression he considered himself superior to the Torah's laws would never happen again. Except for one involuntary encounter with an afflicted individual (the paralyzed man lowered through the roof, analyzed below) Jesus never again performed a healing. He would never do them again, and he never did.

In sum: Despite the artifice at work in the "Temptation on the Temple mount," the passage does not show Jesus was superior to the devil. This bizarre, early Gospel fabrication, incoherent though it is, has concealed Jesus' contemplated suicide as he sought desperately to atone for any inclination to exalt himself as God's anointed messiah. The satanic voice of his unknown father which he feared had caused him, albeit unintentionally, to mislead others to believe in him as having divine authority, had to be eliminated. In fact, Jesus' world was crumbling as he sought John's redemptive immersion.

Jesus' baptism by John

Matthew 3:1; Mark 1:1; Luke 3:1; John 1:1:19-1:51

Note: Because baptism is a central ritual in contemporary Christianity, a brief differentiation between its theological meaning in Jesus' lifetime–and the meaning after his death, up to the present is as follows: After Jesus died, the immersion ritual was made a literal imitation of his entombment and resurrection, with the "holy spirit" transforming the baptized individual from an "unsaved" to a "saved" state. Baptism, to the postmortem Christian was (and is) the enactment justifying Jesus' death by reliving it through "drowning" and then entering the world renewed with an immortal soul.

Logically, Jesus' own baptism could not have had that purpose. Furthermore, Christianity's explanation for the event–that it was an example to others–is unsustainable as an assertion. Excepting Matthew 28:19, a transparently postmortem emendation, Jesus never advocated baptism verbally nor taught its value.

Desperately, Jesus sought John's lineage-purification mikveh (later termed a "baptism"), a Jewish tradition of ritual purification, hoping it might be a path of return to the People and the Covenantal fold.

<u>A brief history of the mikveh as a historic antecedent of what would become the Christian baptism:</u>

Not long after Jesus died, the baptism became a Christianized version of the much more ancient Jewish ritual-immersion in flowing water–called a "mikveh." Historically, the Jewish people had, for at least a millenium before Jesus, made it a practice to bathe in flowing water before entering areas of worship, especially after touching any sources of possible contamination (for example, unclean food, mold, the environs of a cadaver, such as a cemetery, diseased individuals, discharges from maladies, sexual activity or menstruation).

Probably because infection, disease and death had been identified as consequences of poor hygiene, cleansing water was equated with a blessing from God which warded off such evil forces (which we call germs). Therefore, as a model of the ideal world to come, ruled by God and filled with His Presence, the Temple was kept free of all odious contaminants–including unwashed worshippers, as they prayed, yearning for a sacred, new time when life would fully triumph over death.

In the mid-fifth century BCE, the prophet Zechariah envisioned God's return to earth, as in the days of Moses, when once again, the Divine Presence would inhabit the new Temple (the first had been destroyed seventy years earlier by the Babylonians). Prophesying it would occur on a great Sukkot, he described the cleansing of every house and cooking pot.

In this context, we may appreciate that individuals travelling from the north, dusty after their long three-day journey, would often accept John's ministrations and blessing just before ascending the Temple mount. Not only were they preparing to enter the Temple precincts, but on Sukkot, were cleansed for the possibile advent of God's Kingdom.

Meanwhile, Pietists and Temple officials had apparently taken notice of John's prophet-like appearance, especially his odd attire of camel's hair coat and a wide leather belt (Mark 3:4). Further, his call to repentance seemed a false pretense, as if he were personally ushering in God's Kingdom. When he espied them monitoring his immersions,

John did not, however, defend himself–but spoke up for those pilgrims to whom he beckoned. Conjecture suggests among them were many inappropriately dressed for the festival, perhaps not wearing phylacteries or fringed garments and their speech most likely was in an odd Aramaic dialect. Perhaps one might tell they were poor northerners by their worn sandals and simple garments. In other words, like Jesus' disciples, they were regarded as people who had little Torah education and in the eyes of the Pietists, were marginal Jews.

Several thematic segments of the text, analyzed below, are formulations which help illuminate the episode:

1. John welcomes Jesus with the familiar idiomatic Aramaic, "dodi," which may mean "beloved" or "my cousin" in a shortened version of "ben-dodi." In the Gospel rendering, John awkwardly offers no greeting at all, and it is God who hails Jesus as his "beloved" Son (Matthew 3:17 and //'s). For John not even to say "shalom" on the occasion of the festival, tests the credibility of the Christianized account, given John's mother, Elizabeth, was Mary's aunt, and they were indeed very close cousins.

2. Jesus meets a number of his disciples who had gone ahead from the Cana party. They include Andrew, Simon, Philip and Nethanael (probably recognizing him as a resident of Beit Zaida and friend of Simon's). In John 1:35 we also read, "John stood there with two of his disciples." Perhaps they were the Zebedees, and others could have been on hand or proceeded to the Temple mount.

3. Jesus upon being immersed and rising from beneath the water has a sense of being re-Covenanted ("my son") feeling that God has blessed him as purified from his unknown father and any ancestral sin. (Note: This is the same blessing given Solomon who was born from David's adultery with Batsheva; I Chronicles 22:6.)

4. Perhaps some time, even a day or two, after his immersion, Jesus tells the present disciples, "come see (the sukkah) where I am staying" (John 1:39).

[Before turning in greater detail to Jesus' baptism, the reader should be familiar with the three requisite discussions (above): 1. The Kfar Nahum "exorcism" 2. The wedding party at Cana 3. The temptation on the mount.]

Analysis

In the gospels of Matthew and Luke, John reacts to the judgmental onlookers, saying: "Do not presume to say to yourselves, 'We have Abraham as our ancestor'–for I tell you God is able to raise up descendants of Abraham from these stones" (Matthew 3:9, Luke 3:8).

Unmistakably, John rejects their opinion that only those of known Hebrew lineage are worthy of God's coming Kingdom. Local Galileans who made the pilgrimage, even if their family history had been defiled by sins of idolatry, intermarriage with foreigners, adultery, rape, incest, or murder could become fully equal as descendants of Abraham, if it was God's will. Repentance, as John proclaimed, could purify a tainted family tree. Additionally, the holy spirit, according to Jewish tradition (see earlier discussion) was a lineage-purifying intervention from God prophesied to precede the Kingdom.

"Bear fruits worthy of repentance," John calls out to the approaching Galileans (Matthew and Luke 3:8).

What does this mean? He is not talking about food offerings to the Levites or Priests, inasmuch as this was the Sabbatical year (31 CE, just fifteen days after the shemitah began) and harvest was prohibited. Rather, John was referring to the "good deeds" they would bring God as proof of their righteousness. (Note: the Greek original, "poieo"=bear, may also mean "make" or "produce.")

In so doing, as John averred, they could be lineage-pure and have a path to God's Kingdom.

The assertion that "bearing fruit (doing deeds) worthy of repentance" is linked to lineage purification is supported by Jesus' own teaching. Jesus says: (Matthew 7:17. 12:33; Luke 6:43) "The tree (lineage) is known by its fruit...no bad tree bears good fruit...each tree is known by its fruit." In other words, lineage is recognized by the righteousness of the individual. Furthermore, according to John's words, even a tainted lineage could be restored by God if the individual "brings fruit" (does deeds) worthy of repentance.

Having argued that Jesus was on the verge of suicide (see "Temptation on the Jerusalem Temple mount," above), after learning he was born from adultery, we now understand that he sought lineage purification by John's immersion.

At stake was not only Jesus' Covenantal legitimacy, but his very eligibility to share in the Kingdom of God when it became manifest. Reflecting on his evil inclination (yetzer ra) originating with his unknown father and his mother's adultery, he questioned his own motives. Perhaps (as noted above), he had encouraged his disciples to revere him. Did he hope to rule them and others by acting as if he were superior to Torah—or lead them to think that its commandments didn't matter? Had he let them believe he could forgive sin and was God's equal?

The evidence he experienced these doubts is at the core of the devil's dialogue in the Gospel version of the temptation scene, elucidated in the prior discussion. The devil is the one offering Jesus the chance to "rule kingdoms." Having extracted the truth that Jesus was suicidal over his possible sin, we now may appreciate the drama of his baptism.

Realizing that he was possibly in "exile" from the Covenant, Jesus found hope in John's exhortation to repent, followed by the relevant words of the prophet Isaiah (Isaiah 40:3-4):

> "Repent for the Kingdom of God is at hand. A voice calls out. Make a way for God in the desert. Pave a road in the wilderness for our God. Let every valley be lifted and every mountain and hill made low. Let the rugged ground become level and the ridges become a plain. The Presence of the Lord shall appear and all flesh as one shall behold."

Closely examined, this Isaiah passage is about lineage-defilement and Covenantal exile, with the prophet's words promising possible redemption.

Here is the translation of the Hebrew original into the Gospel English version, based on the Greek original:

> "The voice of one crying in the wilderness: Prepare the way of the Lord, make his paths straight (Matthew, Mark and Luke) and continuing in Luke 3:5 only: "Every valley shall be filled and every mountain and hill shall be brought low, and the *crooked* (my italics) shall be made straight, and the rough ways shall be made smooth; and all flesh shall see the salvation of God."

The use of "crooked," is significant. In fact, the word "crooked," based on a Hebrew equivalent ("akov") is discussed by Rav Simeon ben Menashe in the Talmudic passage, Hagigah 1:7, stating: "What is that which is crooked and cannot be made straight? He that has intercourse with one forbidden and by her begets bastard offspring..."

Still, it is necessary to inquire whether the meaning attached to the term by the early rabbis was shared by Luke, in declaring, "the crooked shall be made straight."

In the original Hebrew of the Isaiah passage, "crooked" is a translation of the word "akov." However, elsewhere in the Torah "akov" is translated as "rugged." In fact, "akov" and a variant, "akuv" do have another meaning. Respectively, the former may refer to something insidious and the latter to a genealogical relationship, identifying who is descended from whom. Etymologically, the words are related to the heel of the foot, implying one follows the heel (is descended from) another, and by association was thought of as a protuberance, in that the heel "sticks out," being a bump on the foot.

Ironically, it is the Gospel translation of the Hebrew into the Greek which preserves the meaning of the original Hebrew. The Greek "skello" means "crooked," "perverse," or "wicked," and therefore is about the character of people more than about terrain and topography (as is "rugged").

Therefore, when John quotes Isaiah saying, "the rough ways shall be made smooth," it is the symbolic equivalent of: "Progeny descended from sin will be restored to the Covenantal path."

Based on this analysis, we have corroborated the assertion that John's immersions were intended (at least in part) for people Covenantally exiled by the "bump" in their otherwise smooth Hebrew lineages.

And there is one more conclusive piece of evidence that Jesus' baptism was intended to purify his sin-tainted family history. The Isaiah passage, his call to sinners to be immersed "for the forgiveness of sins" (Mark 1:4), when read in synagogues was accompanied by the reading of Deuteronomy, chapter 7. The Torah text is concerned with forbidden marriages and explicitly warns against intermarriage with foreigners of idolatrous nations. The progeny of these marriages belong to the category of lineage-defiled offspring. Therefore, the exile from which Isaiah envisions return, was not only geographical (from Babylon) but, was Covenantal, on God's Day anticipated to end spiritual defilement caused by intermarriage with idolatrous foreigners.

In conclusion: Jesus' baptism was his attempt to achieve purification of his sinful lineage—and to be a recipient of God's Spirit—so that he might teach according to His will, repenting the impression he gave of having divine powers.

Here then, is the broad brush-stroke sequence of events during the time Jesus arrived in Jerusalem for the Feast of Booths, in the month of Tishrei (October) of 31CE.

1. Distraught that he has possibly been guided by an evil voice of his unknown paternity, Jesus considers suicide. "Temptation on the Mount," analyzed above.

2. Desperately, he seeks John's lineage-purification mikveh, the "baptism- immersion" to return him to the People and the Covenantal fold. John greets him as his cousin (John's mother, Elizabeth, was Mary's aunt) and declares: "God can raise up descendants of Abraham from these river stones," and immerses him.

3. Jesus finds hospitality in one of the Sukkot huts always receptive to guests. Jesus says to several disciples who had gone ahead from the Cana party (John 1:38-1:39): "Come see where I am staying." They include Andrew, Simon, Philip and Nethanael (probably recognizing him as a resident of Beit Zaida and friend of Simon's). In John 1:35 we

also read, "John stood there with two of his disciples." Perhaps they were the Zebedees, and others could have been on hand.

Don't think I wish to abolish Torah...

Matthew 5:17-5:19

Aware his own disciples showed him excessive reverence, and might well have fanned the rumor of his divine powers, Jesus finally declares, following his purification by John in Tishrei of 31 CE:

> "Think not that I have come to abolish the Law (Torah) and the (Neviim/books of the) prophets; I have not come to abolish them but to fulfill them. For truly I say to you, until Heaven and earth pass away, not an iota (in Hebrew a 'yud' which is the smallest letter), not a dot (referring to a 'tittle,' a small graphic flourish at the top of various letters in the Torah) will pass from the Torah until all is accomplished. Whoever then relaxes the least of these commandments and teaches men so, shall be called least in the Kingdom of Heaven. But he who does them and teaches them will be called great in the Kingdom of Heaven."

That Jesus' Gospel pronouncement preserves much of what he actually said, cannot be disputed. In that it is thematically contrary to dispensing with Torah, and offers no viable basis for Christian theology to end Torah law, proves it was included in the New Testament because these were words he was known to have spoken. Therefore they could not simply be deleted (an observation also made by Giza Vermes).

To make it palatable to the new theology, however, editorial modifications were introduced suggesting an alternate meaning.

As the text explicates, three criteria are mentioned as the time when Torah would become passe: a. When Jesus "fulfills" Torah b. when heaven and earth pass away and c. until all is accomplished.

A traditional Christian, based on the Gospel text, sees Jesus' statement as anticipating a time when Torah will have been fulfilled (by him) and all in it "accomplished." After the anticipated "fulfillment" takes place, according to such a view, Torah is essentially passe as a body of law, valued only in its message concerning right and wrong (that is, the Ten Commandments, loving God, loving your neighbor, and the prophetic suggestions about justice, and the coming messiah). As to the end of "Heaven and earth," a Christological view must regard that as having perplexing significance.

Did he mean that the earth, sun, moon and stars would cease to exist, after which Torah would no longer apply? Was he saying that such a cosmic catastrophe was to accompany the revelation of his own messiahship?

If he meant such a thing, his disciples and the apostles—as well as all members of the early church were ignoring his declaration—since they proceded to change and abandon Torah after he died—without any astral annihilation occurring.

This issue, I propose, was facing the Gospel editors as they framed the text.

To obfuscate the cosmic timeframe, intending, it seems, to provide a basis for dispensing with Torah soon after he died, they apparently attempted a midrashic coverup, adding the other criteria: "I have come to fulfill the (Torah's commandments)" and, "until all is accomplished."

In John 19:30, the words "It is accomplished" are represented as the last ever spoken by Jesus as he expired on the cross. As the only Gospel text claiming these were Jesus' last words, we are on reasonably safe ground to assume they are the appended corroboration that with his death, Torah observance may in large part be abandoned (as per Matthew 5:17-5:19).

Without adding "until all is accomplished" to the words actually spoken by Jesus, the Gospel agenda was facing a conceptual crisis. The fledgling theology depended on faith in Jesus—not observance of Torah tradition—to provide enlightened righteousness and salvation. If Jesus was to be the Christ of Christianity, "until all is accomplished" was necessary.

Jesus' death thus became the Christianized, determinant event for ending sanctification of Torah.

Having hypothesized that the words, "I have come to fulfill them... until all is accomplished" do not belong to Jesus, but were inserted to justify an end to Torah tradition (a position fully argued farther on), we may now make the following surmise: the words "until heaven and earth pass away" were original. In fact, because Jesus actually spoke them, Gospel editors found it critically important to add, "I have come to fulfill them...until all is accomplished." Otherwise, standing on its own, the phrase, "until Heaven and earth pass away..." would have required Torah observance after Jesus' death.

Central to this discussion, are the following assertions:

1. Based on the fact there was no astral calamity, not during his life or after, one may infer his followers changed and rejected Jesus' instruction by declaring Torah law passe.
2. The phrase, "until Heaven and earth pass away," is an idiom accessible in Hebrew texts extant during the period, enabling us to fully grasp whether it had genuine apocalyptic and temporal implications. (As we shall see, it was actually a vernacular saying equivalent to our modern phrase, "when hell freezes over"–meaning never.

Since Christianity turns to the prophets to illuminate Jesus' ministry as the fulfillment of scripture, we should expect to find reference to the passing away of Heaven/the heavens and earth in their visions–if it were an established Hebrew perception. According to the classical Hebrew prophets, however, Heaven and earth would never pass away.

The home of God (Amos 9:6 "He who built His chambers in Heaven...") was an unlikely place to suffer such a catastrophe. In prophetic tradition, cosmic signs and wonders trumpeting the advent of God's Day were not equated with the destruction of Heaven, but a display of God's power, His dominion over the heavens. Perhaps because the Hebrews had shown too much reverence for the astral bodies, as if they shaped destiny, God chose to demonstrate their impotence compared to His power. But the heavens in these visions were "shaken" and "disturbed"–not destroyed nor brought to an end.

Here are versions of several prophets' apocalyptic vision:

> "In that Day the Lord will punish the Host of Heaven... then the moon shall be ashamed and the sun shall be abashed. For the Lord of Hosts will reign..." (Isaiah 24:21-23)

Joel reads (3:4-3:5; 4:16):

> "Before the great and terrible Day of the Lord, I will set portents in the sky and on the earth. Blood and fire... the sun shall turn dark, and the moon turn bloody. But anyone who acknowledges God will be among the survivors...(though) the earth tremble, the Lord will be a shelter to His People, a refuge to the children of Israel."

According to Jeremiah (10:2; 30:7-9; 30:11):

> "(God says to you, Israel)...do not be dismayed by portents in the sky. Let the nations (non-Hebrews) be dismayed by them...that Day is awesome. There is none like it. It is a time of trouble for Jacob (the children of Israel). But (they) shall be delivered from it...(and) serve the Lord their God and David the king whom I shall raise up for them...(to Israel): I will not make an end of you. I will not leave you unpunished, but will chastise you in measure..."

The prophet Ezekiel, in his vision of an apocalypse, describes the final battle (38:19-23, selectively):

> "On that Day...mountains shall be overthrown, cliffs shall topple...I will punish him with pestilence and bloodshed, and...hailstones and sulfurous fire. Thus will

I manifest my greatness...in the sight of many nations...
the inhabitants of Israel will despoil those who despoiled
them..."

Zechariah, one of the last of the classical prophets, even provides a
numerical estimate of the losses on God's Day, saying (13:8):

"(In that Day) two-thirds shall perish...one-third survive
and...I shall declare, 'You are my People.'"

From these varied examples, it is clear that the prophets, however
harsh their vision of God's "Day," did not see His divine wrath as
bringing the creation to an end. Therefore, Jesus' phrasing, suggesting
that Heaven and earth would pass away before Torah was discarded, was
a literary expletive, not the prophesied beginning of God's Kingdom.

From what literary source could Jesus' parlance have come, when
he spoke of the end of Heaven and earth?

In fact, there was a popular Jewish concept that existed, but in so
remote a future was it projected, that it was mostly of interest to an
esoteric circle—and played only a marginal role in mainstream Jewish
tradition. As the following analysis will show, reference to the imaginary
apocalypse had come to mean something that would never happen.

How can one be sure?

First, nowhere in the Gospels is Jesus quoted as saying Heaven and
earth will end when the Kingdom of God commences. In fact, the
Gospels' references to a cosmic upheaval strikingly resemble those of
the prophets indicated above. Mark 13:24-13:26 states: "The sun will
be darkened and the moon not give its light and the stars will fall from
Heaven and the powers in the heavens will be shaken..."

(For similar descriptions, see: Matthew 24:7; 24:29, Mark 13:7,
Luke 21:11; 21:25).

Assuredly, even these cosmic "shakings" (which did not terminate
Heaven or the earth) were inserted by postmortem devotees, most likely
Jesus' disciples. His own concept of the Kingdom's advent rejected the
very notion of signs—cosmic or otherwise. Mark 8:12, quoting Jesus,

puts it this way: "Why does (everybody) seek a sign? Truly, I say to you no sign shall be given to this generation..." (parallel statements in the Gospels: Matthew 16:1-3; 12:39, Luke 11:29).

Furthermore, Jesus, in saying "this generation," did not mean the Kingdom of God would occur in the far off future. To the contrary, he says: (Luke 9:27, parallels Mark 9:1, Matthew 16:28): "There are some standing here who will not taste death before they see the Kingdom of God."

His saying that there would be no signs—raised the question how would his followers know the Kingdom of God was happening. Their urgent request that he answer that question proves he never envisaged the Kingdom as concomitant with astral wonders—and certainly never suggested a complete end to Heaven and earth was on God's calendar. If he had, the disciples would have spent sleepless nights terrified that their world was soon to be utterly destroyed.

Luke 17:20-17:21 completely rejects all "signs": "The Kingdom of God is not coming with signs to be observed," Jesus said. "Nor will (people) say, "Here it is! Or there it is! For the Kingdom of God is in the midst of you."

Jesus' further attempt to evoke an image of the coming Kingdom is extremely revealing.

"The Kingdom of God," he told them (selectively) "is like a mustard seed...the smallest of all the seeds on earth and puts forth large branches so that birds of the air can make nests in its shade" (Matthew 13:31-32, Mark 4:26-32, Luke 13:18-13:19).

As the one attempting to "plant the seeds," which symbolized Torah interpretation and tradition, Jesus expected the Kingdom to be populated by individuals made righteous by observance of Torah.

Indeed, he says so (Matthew 19:16-17): "If you would enter (life/the Kingdom of God), keep the Commandments" (Parallels: Mark 10:17-19, Luke 18:18-18:20).

Because the Gospels (and Christian theology) sanctify the words "until Heaven and earth pass away," as if they are literal, this study is obliged to further illustrate how far into the mythical future the fringe Jewish circles projected the cataclysm.

From the time of Ezekiel, about 600 BCE until "Daniel" (A pseud-epigraphic authorship) written circa 160 BCE, a demonstrable change had occurred in Jewish apocalyptic circles. The great prophet of the Exile, Ezekiel, had (as mentioned earlier) imagined a final war by God against evil followed by the People beginning an ideal Judean life with a Davidic king as ruler/administrator. Ezekiel had sequenced the apocalyptic events as follows: 1. Cleansing of sin and restoration of living Hebrews to their reunited land 2. those Hebrews who died (presumably in exile) would be resurrected from their graves and rejoin the living Hebrews in Israel /Judah. 3. God would utterly destroy Gog— the symbolic Prince of Evil in an apocalyptic battle 4. A Davidic king (perhaps the resurrected David) would rule over the united country, prosperous and peaceful.

Compare this to Daniel about four centuries later:

1. In the Book of Daniel, there is a penultimate war waged by a temporary, non-Davidic messiah-king. Very likely, this seemingly abstract, symbolic "vision" is rooted in the reality of the Hanukkah War—with the occupation of Jerusalem and desecration of the Temple. The "anointed-one" fights to restore Jerusalem and in Daniel 9:26, after 70 weeks, he is cut off and "is no more."

2. Following his apparent death, the last wars/battles witness Jerusalem being conquered (Daniel 11). Then, with heavenly help from the angel Michael, the People are finally to be redeemed. The time frame indicated until the Kingdom of God begins is 1,290 days (12:11). In other words, the mortal messiah expires after about 490 days of battle, and the next 800 days witness the climactic end of the final war, concluding with God's Kingdom.

3. Next, "many of those that sleep in the dust will awake, some to eternal life, others to everlasting abhorrence" (Daniel 12:2). In Daniel's "arrangement," resurrection of the dead precedes a "Day of Judgment" with redemption of the righteous, and purgatory, the fate of the evil ones.

4. Following the end of the Hanukkah War (indicated in coded language), and the Day of Resurrection/Judgment, the Kingdom commences. Daniel is informed in his vision: It will last "for a time, times, and half a time" (12:7).

No mention is made in Daniel of an apocalyptic end of earth and heaven, nor of a Davidic messiah—but this is the earliest scriptural introduction of a "Two-Kingdom" concept. The first will conclude after "time, times, and half a time" and then, there will be some sort of "second Kingdom." As we shall see farther on, its onset was to occur—according to various esoteric texts of Jesus' era—with an actual end of heaven and earth.

In the era following the appearance of the Book of Daniel, perhaps spanning the first century BCE to the first century CE, marginal Jewish theorists devoted themselves to decoding his numerological references to the "End of Days." Those esoteric Jews who studied Daniel in the first century speculated on the duration of God's First Kingdom (time, times and half-a-time) before a true "End of Days."

Known disparagingly in the Talmud as "machshavey kitsim" (calculators/ponderers of the end of time), their searching for secret revelations in the visions of the prophets and Daniel, as well as other Biblical texts, earned them limited appeal, perhaps like astrology in our own time.

Keeping in mind the issue—namely, whether Jesus was anticipating the actual end of heaven and earth and with it the end of Torah, we would expect mention of that astral apocalypse to be found in the Dead-Sea Scrolls.

Again, even with such elaborate efforts to prepare for the advent of Divine rule on earth, the future envisioned by the Dead Sea sect contains no prognostication of a complete end of heaven and earth.

Rather, the above excerpts show that Jesus' reference to heaven and earth "passing away" was a sardonic idiom based on a familiar—if not widely accepted view—that (unlike the prophets' vision of cosmic portents) there would be a complete end to heaven and earth at the onset of Daniel's "Second Kingdom."

Further, we have evidence that were one to have actually contemplated such an ultimate apocalypse, the time-frame was cosmic.

Here is a sample of a passage in the Fourth Book of Ezra. It reads:

"My son the messiah shall be revealed with those who are with him and those who remain shall rejoice four hundred years..." Comment: To be clear, the four hundred years would be the length of Daniel's first, mortal warrior-messiah, though Daniel had said he would do battle 490 days, not years.

"And after these years, my son the messiah shall die...and all who draw human breath...and the world shall be turned back to primeval silence for seven days as it was at the first beginnings, so that no one shall be left. And after seven days (taken from Leviticus) the world which is not yet awake shall be roused and that which is corruptible shall perish..." and (7:39-42 further relates): "There will be no sun or moon or stars..."

Similarly, the First Book of Enoch (91:15) states: "The first heaven shall pass away and a new heaven shall appear..."

IV Ezra (7:22-24; 9:31-37) also associated the End of Days (as the curtain falls on the First Kingdom) with reverence for Torah. "God strictly commanded...and they ignored His ways. They scorned His Law and denied his Covenants. They have been unfaithful to His statutes... For lo, I sow my law in you and you shall be glorified through it forever... the Torah does not perish, but remains in its glory."

By contrast, only occasional references to Daniel's Second-Kingdom apocalypse turn up in more traditional Jewish texts.

For example, according to Pirke R. Eli i: (At the end of the first Kingdom) "Heaven...shall be folded together like a book...and unfolded..."

According to R. Joseph (Talmud, Nid 61b), only after the end of the first Kingdom, when the souls of those judged righteous were resurrected to live forever, would there be a new beginning (the Second Kingdom). Then and only then, according to R. Joseph "all ceremonial laws would be brought to a conclusion." Notably, as in Daniel, the "End of Days" (that is, the end of the First Kingdom) did not usually entail an apocalyptic battle—nor cosmic signs and portents. Those were to occur at the outset of the first Kingdom.

Therefore, one may conclude, if Jesus had meant literally what he said about Heaven and earth passing away, anticipating its actual occurrence, Torah, based on the above passage, would be sacred until the end of God's Kingdom—hundreds of years, if not millenia off in the future.

As R. H. Charles put it: "When (Jewish) apocalyptic passed over into Christianity it abandoned this (eternally valid) view of the Law and became anti-legalistic."

These examples illuminate the apocryphal context which led to Jesus saying, "until Heaven and earth pass away..." His idiomatic reference was to the apocalyptic, cosmic cataclysm only very few obscure Jewish fringe circles imagined. Unlike the heavenly upheavals which the prophets (and many mainstream rabbis) envisioned as a prelude to the First Kingdom—the complete astral annihilation to commence with the Second Kingdom aeons away belonged to the bizarre mental province of a miniscule sect.

Though the disciples/apostles' decision to set Torah aside without "heaven and earth passing" was contrary to his teaching, Jesus was deemed to have given his followers coded approval to do so. In saying, "until all is accomplished" he had supposedly revealed to them that his death and resurrection heralded the end of Torah law and tradition.

However, because Christianity holds Jesus' death and resurrection to be determinant of ending the Torah's relevance, we should find cosmic portents have been stipulated. They are indeed described—and affirm the general argument that Jesus' insistence on revering Torah was only abrogated after the Gospel editors paid lip-service to Biblical signs.

First, the "cosmic signs" are presented as a Gospelic prophesy:

In Matthew 24:7, "there will be famines and earthquakes...(24:13) but he who endures to the end will be saved and this gospel of the Kingdom will be preached...and then the end will come" (see also Luke 21:11 and 21:20).

In Matthew 24:15 they are specifically related to Daniel's vision:

"So when you see the desolating sacrilege spoken of by the prophet Daniel...let those who are in Judea flee to the mountains...for there will be great tribulation such as has not been from the beginning of the world... immediately after the tribulation...the sun will be darkened and the moon lose its light and the stars will fall from heaven and the powers of the heavens will be shaken."

Notably, excepting Matthew, the other Gospels do not name Daniel, leaving the impression Jesus is only speaking his own thoughts. If, in fact, he did say these signs would occur, we may rightly ask whether, in fact, they match "heaven and earth passing away." The answer is they more closely resemble the events described in the Biblical prophecies, those expected to precede the Kingdom of God.

In other words, the Gospels' astral signs say nothing of the complete end of heaven and earth.

What, then, has become of Daniel's "Second Kingdom" in the Gospels? Aware of the problem, Mark 13:20 (see also Matthew 24:22) states: "And if (Jesus) had not shortened the days (of the First Kingdom) no human being would be saved. But for the sake of the Elect (the disciples/apostles) whom he chose, he shortened the days."

In other words, Jesus changed his mind. Instead of ending heaven and earth—and with it the First Kingdom—he decided to bring about the Second Kingdom sooner, declaring he would arrive on clouds as the "Son of Man" to save the worthy.

As for the portents prior to the First Kingdom, they were inserted as Jesus was dying on the cross (Luke 23:44-45), a match for Daniel's mortal messiah, with "darkness over the whole land...(Matthew 27:51) and the earth shook and the rocks were split and tombs were opened and many...of the righteous were raised..."

Despite the editorial acrobatics, the occurrence of the "great tribulation" at the end of the First Kingdom and Jesus' descent from Heaven as the Son of Man, remained unrealized lacunae in the

Christianized apocalypse. Because they never occurred, even to this day, reasons are still expounded for the "delayed parousia."

To recapitulate:

This inquiry has shown what Jesus meant by "until Heaven and earth pass away"– that Torah was holy even until the end of the cosmos. In fact, one may conclude that were the First Kingdom to last only a single day (let alone centuries or millenia) Jesus' explicitly-stated condition for dispensing with Torah, namely an end of Heaven and earth–had not been met. As has been elucidated in this analysis, the esoteric Jewish calculations placed the Second Kingdom so far into the future that he surely used the phrase "until heaven and earth pass away" as an idiom such as "when hell freezes over," meaning never.

Not only had his followers asserted that Jesus changed his mind (using his divine authority to save the "chosen" from a cosmic end to heaven and earth), but as I shall show in a moment, the other Gospels revised his actual language as expressed in Matthew 5:17.

First, another phrase in the Matthew 5:17-19 passage warrants scrutiny: "Think not that I have come to abolish the law and the prophets. I have come not to abolish them but to fulfill them." As noted earlier, only when glossed by the midrashic words "fulfill them" does Jesus seem to disavow eternal Torah and project its continuation just until his mission is completed.

To the traditional Jew, who "keeps" the commandments of Torah, the term "fulfill" is discordant and has a messianic tone. Jesus' actual vernacular is exposed only several lines later (Matthew 5:19) when he avers: "But he who does them (the Torah commandments) and teaches them shall be called great in the Kingdom of Heaven."

"Does them," and "Teaches them" are words found in the Torah itself ("ay-kev"= *follow* the commandments in Deuteronomy 7:12; la-ah-sot=*do them* in Deuteronomy 8:1; v'shee-nan-tam=*teach them* in Deuteronomy 6:7 are several among numerous examples) which echo Jesus' own instruction in other passages of the Gospels.

If one hypothesizes that Jesus never said, "I have come to fulfill them," but told his disciples: "I am here with you (not I have *come*) to teach you to keep the commandments" his subsequent remark ("he who does them and teaches them") for the first time is a coherent, stylistic parallel and truly matches his typical manner of speech.

A further stylistic departure from Jesus' usual literary excellence, is the awkward repetition of the word "until" in the same sentence. The text reads: "Truly I tell you UNTIL Heaven and earth pass away not a yud or tittle will pass from the Torah UNTIL all is accomplished."

As I have argued above, "until all is accomplished" was intended to dispense with the eternal sanctity of Torah. Stylistically, it appears to be a Christologically motivated alteration, and that would, perhaps be sufficient condition for doubting Jesus ever said it. But, fortunately we do have text which supports this inference. It occurs in Mark 13:30. Instead of the word "until" Mark uses "before."

His wording at first sight seems to revise "not a yud or tittle will pass from the Torah UNTIL all is accomplished" (as in Matthew) to "...this generation will *not* pass away *before*...heaven and earth pass away..."(in Mark).

On closer scrutiny, the Markan "before" was not a revision of the Matthean "until" but has actually preserved a fragment of the original version of Matthew 5:17-5:18 from which "before" was deleted and replaced by "until."

Here then is the chronological sequence of key changes that altered what Jesus said —with his actual words now ascertained (#1 and more fully in #4, below).

1. **I tell you heaven and earth will pass away *BEFORE* a yud or tittle will pass away from the Law (Torah).**

   These were the actual words spoken by Jesus in Matthew 5:17, but Mark 13:30 removes Torah as the subject, revising the text to say Jesus' words would last forever. The word "before" still exists as a relic of the original Matthew 5:17.

   And, in Matthew, this is then changed to:

2. **I tell you *UNTIL* Heaven and earth pass away not a yud or tittle will pass from the Law (Torah).** The change of "before"

to "until" suggests Torah will become passe. The use of "until" only once is hypothetical, and is based on "before" being used once in Matthew 5:17 and Mark 13:30.

3. **I tell you *UNTIL* Heaven and earth pass away not a yud or tittle will pass from the Law (Torah) *UNTIL ALL IS ACCOMPLISHED*.** These are the changes likely made to #1 and #2 by the Gospel authors who revised Matthew 5:17. Certainly, the text reflects an attempt to solve the same problem: Jesus' actual words (#4 below) eternalized the sanctity of Torah observance. Once the interpolations are deleted we may retrieve his actual words in Matthew 5:17-5:18.

4. JESUS' ACTUAL WORDS (returning Matthew 5:17-18 to the original):

   Think not that I am here with you to abolish the Torah and prophets. I am not with you to abolish them but to teach you to keep them. For truly I say to you heaven and earth will pass away before a yud or tittle will pass away from the Torah.

Matthew 5:19, which continues his instruction concerning the eternal sanctity of Torah, is all original:

   Therefore, whoever breaks the least of these commandments will be called least in the Kingdom of Heaven. But whoever does them and teaches them will be called great in the Kingdom of Heaven.

Concluding observations:

Significantly, no complete parallel of the Matthean passage exists in the other Gospels. Their effort to obfuscate the original was achieved by fragmenting the source text.

Mark 13:30, a variant of Matthew 5:17, wrestles with the question of what time frame Jesus meant in saying, "Heaven and earth would pass away," answering it this way: "This generation will not pass away before all these things take place...Heaven and earth will pass away but my words will not pass away."

The Gospel writer has Jesus anticipating the Kingdom of God (as in Luke 21:31) saying it is imminent–but preserves the conceptual passing of Heaven and earth, with the accompanying assertion "my words will not pass way." From Matthew 5:18 and Luke 16:17 we may infer that "my words" was originally "the Law (i.e. Torah)" and was changed to describe Jesus' revelation of his divine identity. Amplifying the Christian message, Matthew 34:27 and Luke 17:26 follow Jesus' pronouncement that "my words will not pass away" with images of impending transition, mentioning the "Son of Man" is expected at any moment ("Therefore you must be ready" Matthew 22:34).

By invoking the Son of Man, the imagery "eternalizes" Jesus, describing his words as even more everlasting than Heaven and earth–without engaging the issue of Torah at all.

In Luke 16:17 the changed text further reduces Jesus' emphasis on Torah observance, twisting and distorting his words to say: "It is easier for Heaven and earth to pass away than for one dot of the Law (Torah) to become void."

Luke, in this wording, is describing Torah as an *obstacle* to the Kingdom of God. Entering the Kingdom of God is made difficult by the existence of Torah tradition. It may even require violence (Luke 16:16). First, the sanctity of Torah law must become void! In his fragmentary version, having added the words: "It is easier for Heaven and earth to pass away..." Luke is saying the end of Torah, although a monumental challenge (equivalent to the unimaginable passing away of Heaven and earth) is necessary for the Kingdom of God to occur.

In sum: Jesus' declaration of Torah's eternal sanctity in Matthew 5:17, freed of its Christianizing midrash, is now clarified. Having its dramatic origins at the Cana wedding, it reached a crescendo of his near-suicide on the Jerusalem Temple mount, became manifest as lineage-purification in his immersion by John, and culminated with Jesus' edict not to change even Torah's smallest letter.

[NOTE: Because the above episode has no causal connection to the next, it may have occurred soon afterwards and not before.]

A paralyzed man lowered through the roof

Mark 2:4-2:12; Matthew 9:1-8; Luke 5:17-5:26

Placed in historical context, one should bear in mind the episode occurs not long after the Sukkot Feast of Booths of 31CE. Jesus is with his disciples in the north when he learns of his cousin John the Baptist's arrest and (hypothetically) retreats to Matthias' home to find peace and quiet. It is late fall or early winter and he is no longer healing afflicted individuals. Unwilling to transgress by giving even the appearance of divine authority to forgive sins, he refuses to open the door when visitors arrive carrying a paralyzed man.

The Christianized Gospel text:

Mark 2:4-2:12 reads (selectively):

> "And they brought to him a paralytic (who had been lowered through a hole in the roof) and Jesus said...'My child, your sins are forgiven.' And some of the (Pietists) began to question, 'Why does this man speak like this? It is blasphemy! Who can forgive sins but God alone?' And Jesus (guessing their thoughts) said, 'Which is easier, to say (to the paralytic), 'Your sins are forgiven,' or to say, 'Rise, take your bedding and walk'?"

In the next few lines of the passage, Jesus is described as saying "rise and walk" in order to show his purported "authority as the Son of Man."

Although Matthew and Mark quote Jesus' form of address to the paralytic as "My child" Luke uses "Man." Very likely, "Man" altered the actual "son of man..." far more common, but probably changed to avoid addressing the paralytic as "son of man," a de-exaltation of Jesus as the Son of Man, which was a title intended to have divine connotations.

According to the Gospel text, after Jesus says, "My child your sins are forgiven," his adversaries angrily reject his pretentions. ("He is blaspheming. Who can forgive sins but God?")

As one examines the passage, the words, "Your sins are forgiven" confirms an important hypothesis. Jesus is represented as healing an individual whose affliction is the result of sin—most likely lineage defilement. Any relief he might provide the paralytic is therefore a demonstration of divine authority. If he forgives the man—and indeed has divine authority to do so—we should expect the paralytic to be healed—that is, to rise and walk. After all, Jesus' forgiving him would end his punishment.

But why doesn't that happen?

When the Gospel version relates that Jesus told his critics "Which of these is easier to *say* 'your sins are forgiven,' or say, 'get up, pick up your bedding and walk?' we should realize he means, "Which of these is easier to cause to occur?" In this light we may adduce that, according to the Gospels, the man isn't cured because, as Jesus explains, all he could do was say "your sins are forgiven"—not enable him to get up and walk.

And, did he say, "Your sins are forgiven"?

If he had, and the man didn't walk, his words would have been correctly perceived as making false pretense to divine powers he didn't have. Also, if he had pronounced: "get up and walk" and the man remained motionless, Jesus' adversaries would have mocked him and said, "we told you so." It would have proved to them that Jesus was a fake.

As the Gospel passage is on the precipice of complete failure to deify Jesus, with the paralytic man not being told to get up and walk (Jesus' own words, that it was easier to say 'you are forgiven,' instead) later editorial enhancement attempts to conceal the facts. "I say to you (Jesus supposedly then tells the paralytic) so that you may know that the Son of Man has authority on earth to forgive sins, stand up, take your mat and go to your home…" (Mark 2:10-2:11).

This attempted Gospel remedy for a healing that never happened, not super-imposing—but *conjoining* a messianic "cure" of the paralytic, is itself evidence that the truth required midrashic enhancement to preserve the Christianizing message.

Significantly, its historical core is the transparently non-theologized Jesus.

Then what did he say? Embracing his deeply held belief God's Kingdom would offer cleansing of all sin (see, among others, Jeremiah, Isaiah, Ezekiel, and Joel), we may conjecture he said: "Your sins *will be* forgiven," and in a personal display of compassion and his own human limitations, he expressed a near-maudlin disappointment that this afflicted individual was beyond his ability to help. The hypothetical text states: "It's easier to tell him his sins will be forgiven, than to get him to stand up and walk."

Finally, as noted, had Christianity's version of Jesus' "forgiveness" actually occurred–the cure would have coincided with the words, "Your sins are forgiven." In and of itself that phrase would have been the act of divine intervention enabling the paralyzed man to stand up and exit the house. To better appreciate the validity of this premise, we should compare the episode to one described in the Gospel of John (5:8-9; 5:14-15) "Cure of the sick man at the pool of Beit Zata," a Jerusalem Temple precinct.

That text reads, selectively:

"(Jesus asked the man) Do you want to be well again?...then get up, pick up your sleeping mat and walk. The man was cured at once, and he picked up his mat and walked away...after awhile, Jesus met him in the Temple and said, 'now that you are well again, be sure not to sin anymore.'"

What we may immediately observe is that the man is represented as a sinner, and when Jesus cures him, he is not only enabled to walk, but is forgiven his sins. Therefore Jesus tells him "not to sin anymore." The healing and forgiveness are one and the same event. There is no delay between being "forgiven" and "getting up to walk."

Though this story is a theological invention, the pool-side "cure" is not without historical interest. Almost certainly, its author was familiar with the paralytic lowered through the roof and fabricated a parallel healing with Jesus fully deified, and not needing to regret his human limitation.

Quite likely the Gospel of John, in this passage, is evoking the evolving image of Jesus after he died, equating him with God as his "son." No longer is the passage in the Gospel of John bound by historical testimony as was the paralytic lowered through the roof. Plainly, it is inconceivable that Jesus would say, "I forgive you my son," and the afflicted individual in John 5:8-5:15 not be cured by the words themselves. One can sense that this messianized perspective has come a long way from Jesus' earlier words spoken to the man lowered through the roof: "It is easier to say 'you will be forgiven' than to get him to stand up and walk."

The Hanukkah melee

John 10:22-10:39

Assaulted by stone-throwing adversaries in the Jerusalem Temple courtyard, Jesus declares he has broken no Torah law, and defends the idea a person can be called a son-of-God without claiming to be divine. During this confrontation, the insulting attackers shout, *"No prophet* (and therefore, certainly no messiah) *will come from the Galilee...They are cursed rabble."*

The so-called "cursed rabble" appear to be the "am ha-aretz" of the north, who were a class of culturally ignorant residents who neither knew or cared about the Torah's laws. Their lifestyles created the suspicion they were not pure Hebrews but had defiled ancestral lineages. (See Part One).

Because his attackers echoed the charge that he considered himself the unique son of God, Jesus again felt compelled to end any such perception of him. He would not tolerate further reverence that exalted him over Torah law and Jewish tradition. The "son of God" is a characterization, he says, which has familiar usage in the Psalms (82). For purposes of this study, one takes note that this unpleasant episode is especially remarkable for its lack of Christianizing enhancement. Although one might expect editorial alteration to create an image of Jesus as the only son of God, it apparently preserves his historical response to those accusing him. Accordingly, he replies to the Pietists who would stone him, that he is no different from others described in Psalm 82 whose reverence for Torah have earned them the title son of God. It is a title which, for Jesus, does have special resonance. His lineage-purification is accomplished in a manner parallel to Solomon's, also born of adultery, and who is also called by God "my son."

The parables' biographical context

Jesus' cousin, "John the baptist," had been targeted for arrest by the northern tetrarch, Herod Antipas, as a result of criticizing his wife, Herodias, and faulting their marriage which was a mix of incest and adultery (Luke 3:19-20). According to Jewish law she was still married to her former husband—never having been granted a divorce by him— and he was none other than Herod Philip, Antipas' living half-brother, tetrarch of territories to the north and east of the Galilee.

Despite her marital circumstances, Herodias was approved by the Pietists, who overcame what should have been revulsion at their conjugal consummation. Why were they supportive of their wedlock? Herodias was descended from the original Hashmoneans (Macabees) and was therefore eligible to be their genuine Jewish queen. Moreover, as a prize for their approval, Antipas invited members of the Pietist community to join the inner circle of his administrative council, a role which apparently earned them the title, "Herodians." Assuaging their likely scruples over taking so obvious a political step at the expense of Jewish legal precedent was Herodias' divorce by Roman law. It did not require a husband's consent if granted by judicial authority of the empire, which it apparently was.

Probably before the "honeymoon" was over, John's criticism was reaching a large audience. His followers were many, according to Josephus (Antiquities 18:5) and they were likely stirred by his angry rebuke of the adulterous/incestuous love-nest. Furthermore, not voiced in a vacuum, his harangues justified an attack by Antipas' enemy, the Nabatean warrior king, Aretas. He intended to avenge the humiliation of his daughter, Antipas' long-time Arab wife, Phasaelis, who had fled when Herodias arrived.

Concurrently, Jesus continued his assurance to his circle that they would be welcome in God's coming Kingdom—if they followed the precepts of Torah conveyed in his teaching.

In this milieu, lessons concerning God's miraculous intercession and triumph could only cautiously approach the border of rebellious political speech. The popular hope God would deliver the land and Hebrews from their Roman occupiers lent itself to the expectation of a final apocalyptic war as in Ezekiel, Daniel and tracts of the Dead Sea community—but were ideas best confined to the religious sphere. Crossing it, as had John, risked a charge of sedition. Therefore, following John's arrest, Jesus cloaked his lessons in the literary garb of parables to avoid drawing attention to himself. The Pietists, reacting to his questionable "Covenantal-restoration" agenda might "grind their teeth" —but neither sought nor found a basis in the words of the parables to bring a political charge against him.

Jesus, aware his close relationship to John and continuing vilification might place him in danger, had restricted his teaching almost entirely to parable-lessons.

Earlier in this study, I provided thematic examples which Jesus authored, noting they mainly concerned:

a. Covenantal return of his ostracized students as legitimate members of the Hebrew People, rightfully anticipating equality with other Hebrews in God's coming Kingdom.

b. forgiveness of grudges and financial debts (the main instruction related to Rosh ha-shannah, Yom Kippur —and the Seventh Year, "shemitah," in the tithing cycle).

Various other parables were postmortem, and contain grim warnings of judgment and retribution. They are theological fabrications of Gospel authors/editors and are mentioned in Appendix C., below, to distinguish them as a Gospel genre.

Here, let us consider the biographical significance of the typical, authentic Jesus-authored parables.

The literary style of prose, somewhat akin to a riddle, often presented the listener a challenge. Open to interpretation, Jesus' short morality tales therefore insulated him from the gossip of eavesdropping Pietists, hard-pressed to twist the metaphorical allusions into accusations that he believed himself the messiah. After John's arrest by Antipas in the autumn of 31CE (only about two months after the seventh year shemitah had commenced on Rosh-ha-shannah) Jesus' use of parables becomes so predominant a form of his pedagogy, that his own disciples are bewildered. The Gospel of Matthew puts it this way: "(His disciples asked) why are you talking to them (that is, those onlookers who come to hear him) in parables?" (Matthew 13:10; 13:34). And, "Jesus spoke to the crowd in parables, indeed he would never speak to them except in parables..."

From this narrative, we can infer that Jesus used parables exclusively whenever there was a public setting, with possibly malevolent listeners. Only one explanation makes sense: In their number were, he suspected, Pietists eavesdropping, hoping to hear a lesson that he would soon rule the coming Kingdom of God, subjecting himself to a political charge of sedition.

In Luke 12:1 Jesus says, "Beware of the leaven of the (Pietists and their Herodian ilk) which is hypocricy..." and in Luke 12:53 "(Pietists) were lying in wait for him to catch him at something he might say." "Leaven," was a euphemism for an impurity, by which Jesus meant they were twisting his words and corrupting their intended meaning.

Matthew 22:15 is explicit: "Then (the Pietists) went and took counsel how to entangle him in his talk..."

Quite remarkably, Jesus effort to avoid suspicion had a completely unintended consequence—the disquieting effect the parable symbolism had on his own disciples.

First, at least some among them were confused and unable to grasp their point.

In Mark 4:13 Jesus even asks, rather impatiently, "Do you not understand the parable (of the Sower)? And the Gospel narrative observes: "Privately, he explained all (the parables) to his disciples."

But the disciples conjured a different purpose, believing Jesus had an ulterior motive of intentionally testing them with the parables to weed out the more worthy disciples from those who failed his test of acuity.

According to all three Synoptic Gospels (Matthew 13:11; Mark 4:11; Luke 8:10), the parables were not intended to protect Jesus from treacherous rumor —but to separate the worthy from the unworthy.

Amplified by the parables, Jesus had become the victim of his own well-intended disciples, who, without his knowing it, conjured a king keeping his true identity secret, believing he concealed the coming kingdom he would soon rule behind a glossary of metaphor.

Aware of the danger, Jesus now teaching in oblique, often symbolic prose, would say nothing to even remotely suggest he envisioned the actual political overthrow of Antipas' tetrarchy.

Then, as he and the disciples arrived on the northern side of the Sea of Galilee, Jesus seems inexplicably to explode in a temper outburst, castigating the three lakeside villages which were his usual domicile.

Woes to unrepentant cities

Matthew 11:20-24; Luke10:13-15

As the Gospel text describes the episode, Jesus chooses to condemn three of the local fishing towns on the lakeside shore for their failure to appreciate his divine power and repent. The famous passage begins, "Woe to you Chorazin! Woe to you Beit Zaida...and you...Kfar Nahum (Capernaum)...you will be brought down to Hades."

The image of Jesus suddenly proclaiming himself an unappreciated messiah with divine powers is incompatible with the findings of this study. As we have asserted, the very thought he had caused anybody to believe in him as a messiah nearly led to his suicide.

Then what historic stratum may be recovered from beneath the Christianizing message? And, is there obscure Gospel text elsewhere which may clarify the encounter?

The supposition Jesus was banished from the vicinity of the three lakeside villages, Beit Zaida, Chorazin and Kfar Nahum by their administrators meeting him on the outskirts of their village limits, determined to prevent further disturbance, is an altogether reasonable hypothesis. His disappointment and angry reproach are also what one might naturally expect.

Oddly, one must observe, such administrators are not present when he rebukes the three towns. Further, there are no specific examples of their contempt toward Jesus' "messianic stature" warranting his reproach.

Applying the method of precipitous insight, the supposition he was angry at being banished, is an interpretation which must clarify other obscure text for the passage to rise to the level of a "tested" hypothesis. Obscure until this clarification, such a passage does occur in the Gospels as "The sending out of the twelve." As Christian midrash it grants authority to his disciples to carry on in his name, a motif which was amplified after his death, granting authority to the disciples and apostles to save mankind.

The sending out of the twelve

Matthew 10:5-10 (//'s); Mark 3:19

The text reads (limited selection):

> "These twelve (disciples) Jesus sent out with the following instructions: 'Go nowhere among the Gentiles, and enter no town of Samaritans, but go rather to the lost sheep of the House of Israel. As you go, proclaim the good news, the Kingdom of Heaven is near...he ordered them to take nothing for their journey...but to wear sandals... and not even an extra tunic...then he went to a house."

Until clarified by his banishment in the prior episode, Jesus' need to wish his disciples well, sending them off on their own, has made no sense. Without any place to make his retreat except Matthias' house (presumably) he separates himself from his disciples and sends them off to do good deeds and talk to other Jews about the coming Kingdom.

The Christianizing midrash, what little there is of it, is rather understated, and awkward. In Luke 10:1-10:7 Jesus is described as choosing seventy additional apostles whom he sends out to spread the "good news" and no longer retreats to Matthias' house, but according to Matthew 9:35: "Then Jesus went about all the cities and villages... proclaiming the good news of the Kingdom."

Until now, the traditional Christian has been given to believe, without explanation, that Jesus suddenly chose to go his own way, telling his disciples to fend for themselves. As midrash, the text is Christianized to portray Jesus as giving them the authority to act in his behalf.

Far more mundane than the midrash, as we have now clarified, is the historical reality it enhances. Jesus, banished from the three towns, accepts the fact his disciples will not be held responsible or kept out of their villages because of him. Therefore, he encourages them to make their own way and spread faith in God's Kingdom while he goes to stay with Matthias.

As it turns out, the supposed evangelical drama of their apostolic journey, did not last months or shatter the darkness of the Jewish world with miracles and revelation, but ended rather suddenly with John the Baptist's execution.

As Luke 9:10, observes, "On their return" (when John the Baptist was executed), "the disciples told Jesus all they had done."

Jesus' eulogy for John

Luke 3:19-20; Matthew 14:12; Mark 6:29; Matthew 9:36; John 6:23; Matthew 9:38; Luke 9:49; Matthew 11:11-11:12; Luke 16:16; Matthew 11:18-19; Luke 7:33-34; Matthew 21:26; Matthew 16:24; Luke 11:29; Matthew 12:36; Mark 10:12; Matthew 19:9; Luke 18:11; John 6:15; Matthew 14:22; Mark 6:45

(NOTE: Although this study comprises the first complete biographical sequence of events surrounding Jesus' last years, none is more important than the recovery of the following eulogy.)

Here then follows the account of events never before understood, which commenced with news of John's death.

According to the Gospels, John was buried by his followers (Matthew 14:12; Mark 6:29), and only by the farthest stretch can one imagine his death went without a somber memorial gathering of his many devotees.

The evidence for such an occurrence provides contextual clarity to many formerly obscure Gospel passages. In Matthew 9:36 the narrative relates: "...he (Jesus) saw a great throng and he had compassion on them because they were like sheep without a shepherd."

A "great throng" suggests something special was happening. The description of sheep without a shepherd refers to the loss of a leader –namely John. Were there no other evidence, naturally one could assume the "shepherd" was Jesus speaking about himself, having been apart from the "gathered masses." But, in the Gospel of Mark, immediately following mention of John's burial (6:29-6:30) we read: "The disciples gathered around Jesus and told him all that they had done and taught." They are plainly not the "sheep without a shepherd" to whom Jesus refers.

What was the location when he reunited with his disciples and just then observed the large gathering only a short distance away–and where had he come from? No explicit information is provided, but we do know that his arrival at the site of the "throng" was not by boat. Furthermore, according to the Gospel account, shortly after meeting his disciples, he gets in their boat and goes off with them, presumably a brief excursion where the miracle of feeding the masses loaves of bread and unending courses of fish ensued.

Reassessing the sequence, an actual picture emerges. Jesus arrived at the scene of the "throng gathered without their shepherd/leader" on foot. It was many weeks since his disciples had seen him. (See banishment from the three towns, above, and consequent separation from his disciples, "Sending away of the twelve," when he retreated to Matthias' house.)

Based on his later departure by boat, one may infer he had arrived at the shore of the Sea of Galilee (John 6:23) for the memorial ceremony.

Filling him in on what they had been doing since his absence, one of the disciples exclaims, "Rabbi, we saw a man exorcising demons in your name and we told him not to because he wasn't part of our group" (Matthew 9:38; Luke 9:49).

Responding in a resigned tone, Jesus says, "Don't tell him to stop. Somebody doing things in my name won't be able to say bad things about me afterwards." In this most revealing expression of his state of mind, Jesus appears almost despondent because so many people hate him. He also reveals a desire to avoid gossip that may contribute further to popular contempt.

The stir of the crowd at seeing him is clear. Having had their leader taken from them by an execution tantamount to murder, the gathering is emotionally charged as Jesus addresses them from the water's edge.

His eulogy begins with Matthew 11:11, which reads, "Truly I say to you...there has never been anyone greater than John..."

(Note: I have deleted "born of woman..." because this is a phrase editorially inserted to make John seem an ordinary mortal when compared to Jesus, Christianized as the son of God. Another phrase in the eulogistic soliloquy has Jesus say, "yet he who is least in the Kingdom is greater than he (John)." Oddly discordant with the sentiment of "none being greater than John," the words deserve brief scrutiny. First, they are like "born a woman," belittling John rather than lauding him. Of somewhat greater interest, is the wording, "least in the Kingdom," which recalls Jesus' statement about those who fail to keep the letter of Torah law being "the least in God's kingdom." As analyzed in a prior discussion, the Matthew 5:17-5:19 passage is Christianized to mean Torah law would only be sacred until Jesus' mission (death and resurrection) were completed–so that abandoning Torah (being "least") would be the passport to high stature in the commencing Kingdom. Therefore the phrase "the least in the Kingdom will be greater than he" is Christologically inserted to mean "the one who dispenses with Torah will be greater than John." Luke 16:16 explicitly states that with John's death, the Kingdom has begun–and Torah is replaced by preaching the Kingdom of God.

Significantly, when the phrase "born of woman..." and "least in the Kingdom is greater than he..." are deleted, Jesus' praise of John shows that he did not consider himself superior to his cousin at all.

Apparently, and certainly to be expected, the crowd that day included various individuals loyal to the Antipas' administration, among whom were Herodians (Pietist members of his council), along with representatives of the three towns who had banished him.

As Jesus continued his remarks, he took notice of the adversaries who were present.

"John came to you neither eating nor drinking and you say he was possessed. I eat and drink and you say, 'Behold, a glutton and drunkard, a friend of tax collectors and sinners...'" (Matthew 11:18-19; Luke 7:33-34).

Jesus then said: "When you went out into the wilderness (that is, to investigate and arrest John) what did you expect to see? A reed shaken by the wind? To see a man clothed in soft garments? Listen, those who wear plush clothing live in palaces."

It was an unmistakable castigation both of Antipas and of the Pietists who played an official role as members of the tetrarch's municipal council. Directing his remarks at them, the so-called "Herodians," Jesus decried their investigation of John. As the tetrarch's sycophants, they were nothing more than "reeds shaken in the wind," bending their beliefs to placate Antipas. Therefore, Jesus asks whether they had expected John to be (like them), a reed who would bend in the political wind to maintain a position of authority. Unlike the Herodians, who were ruled by a man wearing plush clothes and living in a palace, John was concerned with God's Kingdom—and he was ruled not by men but by God.

Jesus was, with these words, delineating John's activity from the political realm—arguing that because his purpose was to prepare people for God's Kingdom, his intention could not have been treasonous.

To emphasize his point, he says: "I will ask you a question... the immersion by John, was it authorized by God or by men?" (Matthew 21:26).

Their answer, according to the Gospels is silence. As the narrative explains, they realized, "...if we answer 'from men,' we are afraid of the multitude.'" Any such maligning statement about John's immersions would have been a serious insult to those gathered to remember him.

The narrative syntax follows with Jesus' observation concerning John's execution, that the "Kingdom of Heaven has suffered violence and men of violence have taken it by force" (Matthew 11:12), a straightforward reprimand of the Pietists for their role in John's death.

When one of his Pietist adversaries then challenges him, "With what authority are you acting like this..." (Matthew 21:26) implying he should prove he has authority from God and show a sign from Heaven, he replies, "Why does this generation seek a sign? Truly I say to you no sign shall be given..." adding, "When it is evening you say it will be fair weather for the sky is red...you know how to interpret the appearance of the sky, but you cannot interpret the signs of the times. An evil and adulterous generation asks for a sign..."

In Matthew 16:24 and Luke 11:29 Jesus purportedly adds: "No sign shall be given except the sign of Jonah." Although these words are transparent enhancements intended to theologize Jesus' death as a sign to the Christian faithful, juxtaposing his three days in the tomb with Jonah's three days in the belly of the giant fish, it does have value as a textual link to Matthew 12:36. There, the "sign of Jonah" is preceded by words which may consequently be identified as part of the eulogy: "I tell you on the day of judgment (traditionally preceding the Kingdom of God), men will have to account for every careless word they utter. For by your words you will be (enabled to enter the Kingdom), and by your words (that is, bearing false witness against John) you will be condemned."

About then, having again vilified the Pietists as adulterers (Matthew 11:12), Jesus knew what they were all waiting to hear. Would he, like John, label the tetrarch and his wife, Herodias, adulterers? Jesus well understood the danger of the moment.

Putting himself at risk of arrest —though not immediately for a capital offense of sedition as had John—Jesus' next words were courageous and fateful. "And if a woman divorces her husband," he declared, "and then marries another, she commits adultery" (Mark 10:12).

Notably, only the Gospel of Mark records these words. Matthew 19:9 and Luke 18:11 refer only to Jesus stating a husband could not divorce his wife (unless she was proved to have committed adultery). Almost certainly Matthew and Luke regarded it as illogical to quote what Jesus actually said in the eulogy for one of two reasons:

1. Because if Jesus only repeated what his cousin John had said, meaning Herodias' divorce was illegitimate and she was,

therefore, an adulteress, he would have appeared to be little more than a fugitive from Antipas, sought for arrest because he had said the same thing as John. Antipas even asks: "What is this another John?" If so, Jesus would not match the disciples' image of a messiah on the way to Jerusalem to fulfill God's plan.

2. Because, being contrary to Jewish law, Hebrew wives never divorced their husbands. Therefore Jesus would never have needed to say it.

Fortunately, we have the answer in I Corinthians 7:10-11.

Elaborating on the marital status of women, Paul *quotes* (my italics) what Jesus had said according to Mark 10:12, confirming its historical occurrence. Almost word for word recognizably extrapolated from Mark's passage, the later phrasing of Paul states:

"For the married, I have something to say, and this is not from me *but from the Lord* (my italics): a wife must not separate from her husband—or, if she does leave him she must remain unmarried..."

In the Markan text, Jesus uses the word "divorce" not "separate" and mentions such a woman remarrying as "adultery," a subject omitted by Paul in this context. Paul's deletion of the words "divorce" and "adultery" from the Markan text were apparently due to his disinterest in the Antipas/Herodias scandal which had come to fruition with the tetrarch's banishment by Caligula in 36 CE.

Therefore, Jesus' words in Mark 10:12 are historically reliable, and belong with the eulogistic passages now conjoined. No other person excepting Herodias could have been the target of Jesus' scathing criticism. Herodias had divorced her husband Philip, Antipas' half-brother, by Roman—not Jewish—law. For the purpose of this study, we may assert as a major inference the following: Jesus' accusation of Antipas that his supposed wife Herodias was guilty of adultery—and that her so-called divorce was a sham, was the same insult for which John had been recently executed (Matthew 14:4), his sedition (Josephus: Ant. 18:5:2), largely a pretense.

Here it is altogether incumbent on this author to make the following observation: The courage Jesus showed at John's memorial gathering is truly an example to us all. When he chose to speak out against a woman divorcing her husband, echoing John's fateful criticism of Herodias for her incestuous and adulterous wedlock to Antipas–we bear witness to Jesus' true character. He would not let the cousin who had immersed him in cleansing waters –purifying his Hebrew lineage, and restoring his Covenantal relationship with God at a time of his own personal despair, be a voice silenced. As John had shown faith in the character of Jesus, so Jesus now spoke up for his deceased, beloved cousin, repeating his harsh pronouncement against the tetrarch. It was a decision which he knew could cost him his life.

What happens next continues a dramatic sequence of truly historic proportions. Just before the Gospels describe the famed miracle of providing loaves of bread and fish to the multitude, the Gospel of John 6:15 reports, "Jesus saw they (the followers of John who gathered to mourn him) intended to take him (Jesus) by force to be their king, and he broke free." Matthew 8:18 puts it this way: "When Jesus saw the great crowds surrounding him, he gave orders to leave (by boat) for the other side..."

Properly understood, Jesus had completed his dangerous remarks and turned toward the water, intending to make his way to the disciples' boat not far from shore. As he entered the water (a surmise based on his doing so in the succeeding Gospel text, Matthew 14:22 and Mark 6:45), the assembled crowd heralded him "king," surrounding and impeding his effort to wade to the boat, joining in an immersion that to many likely replicated John's baptisms. As the Gospel of John confirms: They physically forced him to break free and escape their adoring grasp (John 6:15).

Despite his desperate effort to prevent the popular anointing, John's followers, the throng without a shepherd, believed Jesus was the fulfillment of John's prophesy, anticipating a "King" of the People, the one to usher in God's Kingdom. Their faith this was so had been fortified by the many rumors about Jesus' healings, equated by Simon and the others as forgiveness of sin, revealing divine authority to end punishment and suffering. Not long thereafter (see the following discussion), Jesus rebukes Simon for spreading the word he was God's anointed messiah–King of the Jews.

From his Herodian adversaries witnessing the mass immersion, Antipas would hear Jesus was inciting the crowd just as John had done—first, implying he and Herodias were adulterers and then being ceremoniously anointed as they proclaimed him their king.

Jesus' castigation of Herodias for adultery, taken together with his being hailed king, were soon to make him a fugitive, and ultimately become a basis for the capital charge that he identified himself as "King of the Jews." For the insult to his marriage, and especially his wife, the tetrarch would submit to Pilate the charge that Jesus claimed to be king, a capital offense of sedition which satisfied Roman law, providing a pretext for his arrest and execution. As Antipas had explicitly vowed (according to Joanna, whose husband Chuza would have overheard) he would do to Jesus what he had done to John. Although Pontius Pilate had no genuine concern about Jesus, he had a strong political motive for acceding to Antipas' demand he be crucified (elaborated in the concluding discussion).

Jesus becomes a fugitive from Antipas

The "Miracles": feeding the gathered multitude loaves of bread and fish, walking on water, calming rough waves
Matthew 14:13-14:21; Matthew 14:32; Matthew 8:24; Matthew 4:37-3; Luke 8:23-24; Mark 8:10; Luke 8:2-3; Matthew 14:1; Mark 6:14; Luke 9:8; Matthew 14:2; Mark 6:16; Luke 9:9; Luke 13:31; Mark 8:14-8:18; Mark 6:52; John 6:60; John 6:68

It may immediately strike one as discordant that about the same time Jesus rejects the very idea of "signs," telling the Pietists there will be none, he supposedly performs three miracles as signs of his divine identity. Therefore, one may properly inquire whether he changed his mind, or, if not, what is the truth behind the account of the miracles.

From the standpoint of Christian theology, they demonstrate Jesus had supernatural powers equal to Moses (the loaves being equated with manna the people ate in the desert) as well as the famous Hebrew prophets, Elijah and Elisha, who (like Moses), fed the masses from limited supplies of food and parted the water to cross over (II Kings

2:8-9; II Kings 2:14). According to the Gospels, Jesus is imputed even greater powers, walking on the waves and making the water calm. (The comparison of his miracles to ancestral Hebrews is supported by additional detail outside the scope of this inquiry.)

To explore the miracles' possible historical significance, we should first note that the Gospels place them in the following order and context: 1. Jesus joins the disciples in a boat, goes to a place along the lakeshore, and feeds the multitude loaves of bread and fish, turning a small supply into enough for everybody (Matthew 14:13-14:21). 2. The disciples go out in the boat without him—and the water is stormy, the waves high. Walking on the water, he catches up with them. 3. He gets into the boat and the water becomes calm as do the winds (Matthew 14:32).

According to this study's analysis of Jesus' eulogy for John (see prior discussion), having finished his remarks, he retreats from the crowd and their adulation of him as "king," wading to the offshore boat where the disciples are waiting.

In fact, given his outspoken derision of Antipas, he was not only escaping the adoring grasp of John's assembled mourners, he had, from that moment become a fugitive from the tetrarch.

As the Gospel account of this episode was recorded, a major Christianizing decision was at hand. Would the fledgling theology survive if Jesus, instead of possessing divine powers, was on the run and fearful for his life? How would he save others, if he was worried about saving himself?

Faced with the daunting task of explaining why a messiah with divine powers was a fugitive, the Gospel editors dramatized, in midrashic form, the actual historic events which had occurred.

Here is the likely sequence of events which lent itself to the miracle narrative:

1. Jesus' wades to the offshore boat to leave the crowd behind. As they immersed themselves, in the hundreds, the mourners hailed him king, splashing all around him, causing turbulence so that Jesus was "walking on stormy water." (Alternately, his walking alongside the boat, helping to guide it toward shore, in #2 below, may also have been "walking on water.")

2. After rowing awhile, and approaching shore, where the waves were always larger, Jesus jumped out and helped beach the boat without its being swamped (Matthew 8:24; Matthew 4:37-3; Luke 8:23-24). He also may have done this later in the day as they landed on the far side, in Philip's tetrarchy, making their way to Caesaria Philipi. According to the Gospel account, he had calmed the storm.

3. Reaching Magdala, in the area of Dalmanutha (Mark 8:10) just up the lake coast, they were presumably met by Mary (of Magdala) and Joanna—the one character in the Gospels associated with the tetrarch's palace home in Tiberius (Luke 8:2-3). Her husband Chuza, who was employed there as a steward, would likely have told her to warn Jesus, which she apparently did. According to the Gospels, Antipas was informed (probably by Pietist Herodians) about the huge gathering: "Some people were saying John has been... raised from the dead...others said he is Elijah...or a prophet..." (Matthew 14:1; Mark 6:14; Luke 9:8).

Antipas' response (selectively combining Matthew 14:2; Mark 6:16 and Luke 9:9) was: "Who is this about whom I hear such things? John whom I beheaded has been raised from the dead?"

Despite the intent of the Gospels to suggest Antipas was in awe of John's "rising from the dead," even wishing to meet Jesus, the facts prove he was frustrated and resentful and mocked his "return." Plainly, "I beheaded John—and he has been raised from the dead?" was a sarcastic and bitter remark, ominously foreshadowing his effort to do to Jesus what he had done to his cousin.

Luke 13:31 provides Joanna's exact warning to Jesus: "(She) said to him, 'Get away from here. Antipas wants to kill you!'"

(Note: The Gospel of Luke attributes the admonition to "some Pharisees"—the least likely gloss, given the Gospels' constant contempt for them as vicious adversaries. The response by Jesus places the warning correctly. It occurs during the temporary stop in the vicinity of Magdala.)

Jesus replies: "(Joanna) go and tell that fox that I am leaving his region. It is not my intention to die at his hands." As Jesus is fully aware, only if he leaves Antipas' tetrarchy will he have "gotten away" from his jurisdiction.

4. Before resuming his escape, on the shore of Magdala, Jesus and the disciples had lunch, a meal consisting of bread and fish. Searching the wonders worked by the prophets (as noted above), the Gospels found a match to Moses and Elijah who provided bounteous nourishment from very little. Much like walking on water and calming the storm, the "miracle" of loaves and fish was transposed from an actual event: Jesus' words concerning bread, just before they ate.

In Mark 8:14 we read: "Now they had forgotten to bring bread... and Jesus cautioned them, "Take heed of the leaven of the (Pietists/ Herodians) and the leaven of Antipas..." Now a fugitive, he wanted his disciples to refrain from saying anything that could become the source of a false accusation ("the yeast") against him.

It is a very revealing exchange. Jesus is completely preoccupied by what Joanna has told him, having grasped the possible consequence of the report brought from the funeral gathering to Antipas that he was "just like John" –made even more ominous by the tetrarch's wanting to "kill him." When the befuddled disciples respond to his mention of the "yeast of the Pietist Herodians," saying, "We have no bread," Jesus retorts: "Why do you discuss the fact you have no bread? Having eyes do you not see, and having ears do you not hear?"(Mark 8:16-18)

One can hardly exaggerate his frustration, summed up by Mark 6:52:

"For they did not understand about the bread..." to which John 6:60 adds their exasperated confusion: "This teaching (about the bread) is hard –who can understand it?"

Not sensing Jesus' dread, that he was at risk of capture and execution at the hands of Antipas, the disciples ate whatever was brought them by Mary Magdalene from her nearby home. After they finished eating the bread and fish, Jesus told them: "(Go your own way). Foxes have holes and the birds of the air have nests, but I have nowhere to lay my head."

Linked in the Gospel of John to the miracle of loaves, Simon complains that they have left everything to be with him, saying, "Lord, we have nobody to go to" (John 6:68).

[Here, an appended observation is in order. It is of genuine interest that the authors/editors of the Gospels show intermittent awareness of the disciples' shortcomings. Their dull-witted grasp of "yeast" described above, and Jesus' earlier rebuke of their poor literary acumen visa vie the parables, suggests an internal hierarchy based on intellect.

This author is of the opinion that Simon's post-crucifixion leadership controlled five loyal disciples, with Matthias expelled, making a majority of six, including himself. Those entries in the Gospel texts which seem to disapprove of the "ignorant" followers/disciples would therefore be of the other five. See the parable of "The Ten Bridesmaids" as an example. Matthew 25:1]

Concerning the "miracles"

The miracles, as recorded in their postmortem Gospel format, were intended to illuminate Jesus' higher purpose, muting any faithless thought he was making a frightened retreat. His miracles would prove, that contrary to appearances, he had no fear of an earthly ruler like the tetrarch. If he could walk on water and calm the storm, or feed the multitude from meager supplies of bread and fish, no doubt would exist that indeed he was the one envisioned by Hebrew prophets of renown– the messiah king with lineage from David.

As I noted earlier, "midrashim," the literary genre to which the miracle accounts belong, were theological dramatizations of historical realities. The *appearance* to onlookers might be that he was simply wading through choppy water or feeding his gathered devotees from a basket of bread or fish, but to the worthy, the transcendant event was what Jesus was conveying in the act. As recorded in the Gospels, his walking on water and calming the storm, and feeding the multitude from meager supplies of bread and fish, enabled the believer to perceive his divinity even as he "played the role" of a fugitive.

To the disciples and Gospel authors, the miracles were actually very important revelations of Jesus' divine identity, not simply supernatural exaggerations. What might appear to outsiders as ordinary events, were perceived postmortem by the Gospel authors interpreting his life as coded messages from the holy spirit (Jesus' heavenly voice). Those who could "see" Jesus had walked on water, fed a multitude from a few loaves, and calmed the storm were discerning the deeper meaning of his actions and thereby enfranchised as the "elect." Seen through the lens of Christianity, Jesus' behaving like a fugitive, beset by all-too human anxiety and emotional frailties, had been disguising his true identity until the time was right.

The miracles, witnessed by the elect (sometimes a "multitude" of devotees) were, therefore, intended to illuminate Jesus' higher purpose, muting any faithless thought he was making a frightened retreat. By attributing his every action to a messianic agenda, the disciples denied he was simply a man on the run. Whatever had happened, they believed, was meant to secretly instruct the worthy concerning the path to salvation. It was God's program. His human misery, even his crucifixion in Jerusalem, was ultimately to be "justified." Justifying the crucifixion as God's/Jesus' plan was the test of the devotee's worthiness and faith.

Significantly, because the disciples saw everything that happened as a step along his divinely paved path, Jesus' protestations that he was not the messiah fell on deaf ears. Despite his angry rebuke (see the next discussion), the disciples continued to believe their faith in him would win them special stature in God's Kingdom.

The next leg of their journey was to Caesaria Philipi, in Philip's tetrarchy and beyond Antipas' legal grasp. There, Jesus could be sure, the tetrarch's half-brother Philip would hardly be inclined to aid in his capture, given his wife Herodias had left him for Antipas, and that Jesus' supposed crime was denouncing their adultery.

In sum:

When, at John's funeral gathering, contrary to his own instinct for self-preservation, Jesus courageously denounced his cousin's accusers, and called Antipas and Herodias adulterers—he knew he had placed himself at risk. It was a provocative speech which could lead to his arrest on a fairly serious charge of incitement, although it fell far short of a capital offense.

But events took a disastrous turn. The disciples, despite his attempt to dissuade them, had spread rumors he was the anticipated messianic ruler sent by God, sowing the seeds of expectation, and preparing the crowd to proclaim him their king. With the large gathering's words of coronation, "King of the Jews," ringing in his ears, he broke free and made his way to the disciples' boat. Now, he realized, a capital charge of sedition could be brought against him for having a political agenda to replace Antipas. As would shortly be confirmed by Joanna, the tetrarch regarded him as "another John," and intended to "kill him." It did not matter to Antipas that Jesus was an inconsequential threat to his rule, since the extreme charge of sedition was only intended to formally satisfy Roman law, and be the basis for execution—as he sought to avenge the insult to him and his wife. Without doubt, Jesus had every reason to be terrified.

Simon, who do you say I am?

Matthew 7:21-7:23; 14:1; 16:13-16:23; Mark 8:29-30; 8:33; Luke 9:20-9:21; 13:26; 13:31-33; John 6:68

Once he and the disciples landed, and were in Philip's region, Jesus was safe. Even if he had called the Antipas' marriage adultery, he would be ignored by Philip, who also considered Herodias an adulteress for deserting him to fornicate with his own half-brother.

"Peter's profession of faith"

Suspecting that Simon was the source of the crowd's hailing him their king, Jesus found a moment when they were walking alone together, to ask, "Who does everybody say I am?"

(Note: Although the Gospel account of this question says Jesus was asking all the disciples—Mark 8:33 indicates Simon was with Jesus some distance away from the others. Further, only Simon replies.)

In Matthew 16:13-16:23, Simon answers: "Some are saying you are John (that is, resurrected) or Elijah. Others say you are Jeremiah or one of the prophets."

Ominously, these words echo what Antipas has been told (Matthew 14:1).

Not getting the straightforward response he wants, Jesus persists: "But who do <u>you</u> say I am?"

In three Gospels (Matthew 16:16; Mark 8:29; Luke 9:20) Simon answers, saying: "You are the Christ" (literally, savior-king) or in John (6:68) the "holy one of God."

Known to Christianity as "Peter's profession of faith," the historical reality conjures a completely different exchange.

Only a short while earlier, Simon had addressed Jesus as "Lord" (see prior discussion quoting John 6:68 "Lord, we have no one to go to"). Based on Jesus' following diatribe (quoted below), the title, "Lord" made him suspicious that Simon was mostly to blame for propagating his false image as the God-sent king.

Revealingly, the Gospels capture the tone of Jesus' response when Simon says he believes he is the Christ: "But he charged (him) and commanded him to tell this to no one" (Matthew 16:20; Mark 8:30; Luke 9:21).

In fact, if we take this literally, the historic language is well-served. He meant: "Don't say such things about me." The aura of secrecy imparted by the revised, Christianized text, would call for concealing his divine identity in order that he die in Jerusalem as God planned. Matthew 16:21 states: "From that time on Jesus began to show his disciples that he must go to Jerusalem and suffer many things...and be killed."

Again, beneath the Gospels' enhanced version, we may retrieve the historical intent of these words: "They are going to arrest and execute me if you don't stop calling me 'Lord,' or saying, 'I'm your king!'" However, when Simon vehemently declares, "God forbid, Lord. This shall never happen to you!" (Matthew 16:22) we have a response from Jesus that fully confirms this study's reconstruction. He says (Matthew 7:21-7:23): "Why are you always calling me 'Lord' when I tell you not to. No one who calls me 'Lord' will enter the Kingdom of God...many will say to me 'Lord, Lord, did we not prophesy and cast out demons in your name...' and I will declare to them 'I never knew you.'" Luke adds a vivid comment: "You will say we ate and drank with you, and you taught in our company...but I will say I don't know where you come from..." (Luke 13:26, with clarified wording).

[A technical note: Jesus' threat to deny knowing Simon and the others—if they keep addressing him as "Lord" is relocated by the Gospels to a different context, Matthew 7:21. Quite likely, had it been left where it was originally spoken, as quoted above, his rebuke would have been impossible to Christianize. The critical match showing the passages belong together is their identical subject, content, literary style and tone. When Simon calls Jesus the "Christ" (Mark 8:29)—his un-Christianized response is: "Stop saying such things or they will arrest me" which Simon rejects, saying, "Lord, this will never happen to you" (Matthew 16:22). For addressing him as "Lord," in this passage, Jesus is plainly infuriated and calls Simon, "satan" (Matthew 16:23; Mark 8:33). The conjoining of Jesus' threat to disavow all connection to those who call him "Lord" (Matthew 7:21) fits the moment perfectly and is completely unsupported by any other Gospel context.]

No variation can alter his meaning: "If you persist in calling me 'Lord,' you will get me killed."

Having adamantly rebuked Simon for addressing him as "Lord," warning that if he keeps doing it he will even deny knowing him, Jesus has apparently become so disgusted, he doesn't even want him walking at his side. In one of the Gospel's most revealing accounts of his dismay at being labeled the messiah, he tells Simon to get away from him: "Get behind me satan! You are not walking at the side of a god—but of a man"(Matthew 16:23; Mark 8:33). (Note: Thematically, the Christological value of the Gospel's altered version is its implication Jesus intended to die, and Simon simply was hindering his plan to do so. See below for further analysis of the passage.)

A closer look:

Christianizing the text of "Peter's profession of faith"

Perhaps more than any other quotation of Jesus' words, the actual historical text could not stand as spoken if Christianity was to survive. At its very heart, the words were a complete, emphatic denial by Jesus of his messiahship.

Because of its potential to explode the fledgling theology, Gospel authors/editors, presumably the disciples themselves, recast Jesus' words in the mold of Christian belief. It is a literary cover-up of profound consequence.

The attempt to alter the text for theological purposes is first notable in Matthew 16:17 when Simon is no longer rebuked for saying Jesus is "the Christ" but proves himself worthy for having "recognized" his divine identity. As a reward, Jesus chooses him to be the one to transmit heaven-sent ordinances, and have the "keys to the Kingdom" deciding who could and could not enter.

Accordingly, his name is changed to "Peter" meaning foundation stone of the church.

Immediately after Simon tells Jesus he knows him to be "the Christ" Jesus admonishes the disciples "to tell no one."

As developed in Matthew 16:21 and Mark 8:31, Jesus was quieting the disciples so that his secret identity not be compromised by their frivolous talk.

Next, we are informed (in the continuing Christianized version): "And Jesus began to teach his disciples that he must go to Jerusalem... and be killed and on the third day, be raised."

Luke 13:31-33 elaborates the theological message: "I go my way today, tomorrow and the day following. For it cannot be that a prophet die outside Jerusalem."

Whether they addressed him as, "Lord" or had him speak of himself as a prophet, or even, eventually, as the "Christ," all these titles shared the traditional connotation of administrator of God's rule–equated with being "messianic king." Once Antipas could make the charge of sedition based on his followers hailing him their divinely chosen sovereign, Roman law could be applied.

After his death, Jesus was theologically portrayed as confiding the true, secret meaning of his rebuke of Simon for calling him "Lord." In the Gospels' desperately-strained version of his explanation, he must keep a low profile in order to reach Jerusalem before he is arrested. Then, in three days, he will be killed and raised from the tomb. The three-day journey from Ceasaria Philipi to Jerusalem (for Passover) was thus decoded by the disciples to reveal Jesus was not actually talking about that journey at all—but about the journey from death to eternal life.

Almost oddly discordant, just a few lines farther on (Matthew 16:23; Mark 8:33) Simon seems to totally lack spiritual acuity when, having doubted Jesus would ever be killed, is told: "Get behind me satan. You are a stumbling block to me. You're not on the side of God but of men." What had he done that so quickly transformed him from a personal emissary of Jesus in the coming Kingdom—to a hindrance? Apparently, because his words were oblivious to Jesus' secret agenda, that he die, be entombed for three days and be resurrected, Jesus rebuked him for impeding God's plan. The Gospel message had thus turned history on its head so that Jesus' ordained death, no matter how hard it was for Simon to grasp, was God's design.

In this light, any act or statement causing his premature arrest—would be "satanic." To have let stand the actual words, **"You are not walking at the side of a god, but at the side of a man"** (instead of "You are not on the side of God but of men") would have deprived Christianity of its Christ.

Justifying Jesus' death not only became the Christian "test" of the faithful to achieve salvation, but saved the disciples and especially Simon from the awful truth—that due to their coronation of him as messianic King they had unintentionally provided Antipas grounds for arrest under Roman law and abetted the tetrarch in bringing about their teacher's gruesome death.

Jesus' final Passover

(Gospel references are provided in the context of the following discussion)

    a.   **advance arrangements for the ceremonial meal**
    b.   **entry into Jerusalem**
    c.   **the meal ("last supper")**
    d.   **Judas' betrayal**
    e.   **arrest**

f. **hearing before Caiaphas**

g. **judgment before Pontius Pilate**

h. **crucifixion**

i. **entombment, disappearance**

j. **reconstructing what actually happened**

k. **who was Joseph of Arimathea?**

If one wonders why Jesus chose to leave the safety of Caesaria Philipi, a virtual sanctuary outside Antipas' tetrarchy, to go to Jerusalem for Passover, it was a premier event of the Jewish year. Nor, did his decision appear to place him in any great danger. Weighing the risk, he apparently believed his small group would be lost in the crowd of thousands making the same three-day pilgrimage. Furthermore, they would soon reach Jerusalem where Antipas, it could be presumed, had no authority.

According to the Gospels (Luke 9:51), "...as the day of his demise approached, he resolutely set out for Jerusalem...and they entered a village of Samaritans, but were not welcome because they were going to Jerusalem..."

While Samaria was a region between the Galilee and Jerusalem which would have been safe from Antipas—it was not safe from the people who lived there—the Samaritans. Their long history of conflict with the Hebrews was known to manifest itself in violent acts toward Jewish pilgrims passing through.

Though we are not informed more explicitly about their encounter, the phrase "were not welcomed" portrays the Samaritan hostility.

Note: The famed parable of "The Good Samaritan" (Luke 10:29) explicitly contrasts a compassionate member of their community with various Hebrews who are callous, despite their supposed social and spiritual stature. On closer inspection, however, the individual is actually compared to his fellow-Samaritans. Although Christianity has made this parable a basis for asserting the universality of Jesus' mission, his message may be summed up: "Even a Samaritan can transcend his low nature and therefore so can you be more righteous than any Jews who show similar shortcomings."

Following Luke 9:51, Matthew resumes the narrative, informing us: "Jesus left the Galilee and went to the region of Judea beyond the Jordan." Given this text's location in the "approach-to-Jerusalem" section, it clarifies which road he finally took to that fateful Passover festival. He had opted to cross to the east bank of the Jordan River, and join the throng following that popular route. If less dangerous than Samaria, Perea, as the area was called, was hardly safe. It was a district belonging to Antipas' tetrarchy. Aware Antipas' police or soldiers might be on the lookout for him, Jesus very likely did his best to blend in.

Upon reaching Bethany, a village on the outskirts of Jerusalem, he and his companions were welcomed as guests by Mary and her sister Martha. It was a Wednesday afternoon (Luke 10:38-42).

The next morning, Jesus sent ahead several members of his entourage into Jerusalem (Mark 11:1).

According to Jesus' instructions, they were to first go across the way and acquire an adult ass on which they might transport their garments (Matthew 21:7), as well as a younger one on which Jesus would later enter the city. Once they were within Jerusalem's walls, they were to find a water carrier who would direct them to a house with ample space and make arrangements for their festival meal (Mark 14:13-14:16).

To the Christian ear, Jesus' fore-knowledge that they would meet a water carrier who would guide them to a place for their dinner demonstrates omniscience. From a historical perspective, however, Jerusalem's streets on the morning before Passover (beginning at sundown) were filled with water carriers. Their function, in fact, was to supply women with water to dampen the dough for matzah just before baking. By slapping it with wet hands, they were able to flatten the dough properly and this was an activity that took place in the courtyards of clustered houses. The water carriers, as Jesus knew, were therefore familiar with which homes might provide space—as it was custom to invite all pilgrims who came to Jerusalem to use any available room for their Passover dinner.

It is noteworthy that when the disciples ask Jesus where they should "prepare to eat the Passover" (Matthew 26:17), they are explicitly referring to the sacrificial lamb (Luke 22:7-9)– although no mention is made of roast lamb at the meal itself. (Note: Passover in Hebrew, "pesach," means "lamb," which is why the text refers to "preparations for eating the Passover." The later meaning, "to skip over" was adapted to the scene of the tenth plague which skipped/passed over Hebrew homes, in the manner of a skipping lamb, just before the Exodus.)

Why was there no mention of eating lamb at the fateful supper? John 1:29 quotes John (the baptist) as exclaiming, as Jesus approaches, "Look there is the lamb of God who takes away the sin of the world..." Therefore, the Gospel of John, intent on preserving Jesus' transcendental role as the sacrificial lamb–places the Passover a day later–having it begin not on Thursday, but on Friday. According to the Gospel of John, then, the fateful night of Jesus' arrest was not Passover at all. And, the next evening, Friday, when Jesus' died, he could be considered "the lamb." Otherwise, if Thursday evening was Passover, he could not very well have been eating lamb–and, at the same time, be the lamb.

Contrary to John, the other Gospels are all in agreement that Thursday evening was the Passover meal (Matthew 26:17-18; Mark 14:12; Luke 22:7-8). Instead of altering the date of Passover, to avoid contradicting the image of Jesus as "the lamb of God," however, they simply deleted mention of it from the menu.

From Christianity's theological perspective, Jesus' activity has all been leading up to the drama about to unfold. Entering the city gates on an ass in the exact fashion the prophet Zechariah envisioned (Mark 11:9 paralleling Zechariah 9:9), he is thought to reveal his messiahship while adoring attendants shower his path with leafy branches and declare "Hosannah!" that is, "Save us!" (Matthew 21:7-9; John 12:13-12:14). A preeminent influence on the religious thinking of Jesus' era, Zechariah's focus had mainly been on the advent of God's Kingdom. If there were signs his prophesy was coming true, God's Day was at hand.

In their portrayal of events surrounding Jesus' entry into Jerusalem, the Gospels further tell of Judas receiving thirty shekels to betray him. (See Matthew 26:14-16, evoking Zechariah 11:12 and its precedent, Exodus 21:32, establishing Jesus' "value" to his betrayer as equivalent only to a slave.)

Not long after his entry, Jesus is said to turn over the tables of the money changers (Matthew 21:12-13 paralleling Zechariah 14:21).

For our purposes, we must recognize that these Zechariah add-ons are not history. Jesus, contrary to the Gospel view, certainly entered Jerusalem as anonymously as possible, keeping a low profile to avoid attention and any chance of arrest. Assuredly, the last thing he would do was create a public disturbance.

The "last supper"

Before they sit down to the meal, Jesus washes Simon's feet and insists the other disciples do the same for each other. (The text actually says he washed all the disciples' feet–but in John 13:14 Jesus only shows them what to do to each other.)

The narrative of John's Gospel records the moment as a paradigm of "perfect love" (John 13:1), with Jesus instructing them, "I have given you an example so that you may copy what I have done to you."

If one is a traditional Christian, "perfect love" requires overcoming all sense of superiority toward others, using the foot-washing as a model. Commentaries further elaborate the Christian message that the cleansing water was meant to purify the disciples' spirit and prepare them for unity with Christ.

On the other hand, Jesus' own words never provide a clarifying explanation for washing Simon's feet. "You will understand later," he states (John 13:7), admonishing Simon, "Unless I wash you, you can have nothing in common/have no share with me" (John 13:8-9).

Even superficially, one is immediately aware this does not clearly indicate Jesus' intent to teach "perfect love." In fact, if that were the lesson, Simon has apparently missed the point. His reaction is to vehemently resist, saying, "Never. You shall never wash my feet!"

Faced with these thematic anomalies, one may wonder whether the foot-washing episode is historical–or the invention of John's Gospel, in its only recorded occurrence.

A viable assessment of the scene's historicity begins with this fact: A first-century Jew simply did not sit down to the Passover meal with feet dirtied by dust of the ground. Jesus was, therefore, embracing Torah tradition.

Close scrutiny of John 13:8-9 has led to various translations. The three most widely accepted are: (If you don't let me wash your feet) "You can have nothing in common with me," or "You can have no share with me" or, "You can have no part with me."

In light of the tradition, a likely historical reconstruction is: "If you do not (let me) wash your feet, you can not share the meal with me."

The "example" Jesus set, according to this reading, was intended to show them how best to perform the ritual cleansing—and had nothing to do with humility as he "lowered himself" before Simon to perform the menial task. Instead, he demonstrated how to easily accomplish what otherwise would be a difficult and awkward physical effort. Were the disciples to take the basin and do their own feet, they would have to bend completely over, while managing to thoroughly rinse and wipe their soles, toes and ankles. In the process of bending and crouching, their garments could become easily soiled. Nor could they do it by putting their dirty feet up on any of the dining furniture, as that would make whatever was touched unsuitable for use during the ceremonial supper. Hardly a transcendental reference to salvation, Jesus is now understood to have been speaking in the most mundane terms. Oblivious to his purpose, however, and distressed that Jesus is kneeling before him, Simon protests. Using the same vernacular as earlier, when he rejected the possibility Jesus would be arrested and killed ("Lord, this will *never* happen to you!") Simon echoes his intransigent refusal to perceive Jesus as an ordinary mortal, and again exclaims, "Never! You will never wash my feet!"

Jesus, aggravated that his prior rebuke for calling him "Lord" failed to set Simon straight (See prior discussion, "Who do you say I am?"), issues the ultimatum intending to end the disciples' misapprehension of his identity. "If you do not (let me) wash your feet, you can not share the meal with me."

What was to be a lesson in Jewish Torah custom had thus become an act forcing Simon to either accept the fact he was a man and not a god—or be excluded from his company at the Passover dinner.

Judas' betrayal

Having taken their places at the dining table and begun the meal, they are stunned when Jesus announces that one of them who has "dipped from the same dish with me will betray me" (Matthew 26:22-23; Luke 22:23). Not surprisingly, his words are met with denials and complaints as one after the other asks, "Is it I?" best understood as, "Do you mean me?" or, "You think it's me?"

(To take the phrase "Is it I" literally, makes no sense since those who were innocent would hardly have to inquire.)

When Judas asks, Jesus answers: "It is you who has said it" (Matthew 26:25) "...now go and do what you do (that is, intend to do) quickly" (John 13:27).

The phrase, "It is you who has said it" carries significant weight, for though it goes unrecognized by the disciples, it is used by Jesus in three other contexts which shed light on its legal implication. In eulogizing John, Jesus proclaimed: "For their unfounded words of accusation, they (witnesses testifying against John) will be judged by God" (Matthew 12:36). Slightly re-worded, it is the identical legal charge which Jesus makes at the hearing before Caiaphas and subsequent judgment by Pilate (Matthew 26:64; John 18:37): "You have said it," and "It is you who say it." Significantly, he has, in the latter two instances, plainly accused his accusers of bearing false witness against him. (Torah law called for punishing perjury with the same sentence being deliberated or meted out to one falsely accused.)

Repeatedly asserting the legal formula, as I shall show farther on, Jesus was denying what they said about him, namely that he claimed to be the messiah/king.

Christianity, as one may anticipate, sees a different meaning. If he exhibited anxiety about his capture and execution that was to set an example: life might be beset by travail and death—but enduring faith in him as the "Christ" was the path to eternal salvation.

Despite Christianity's omniscient Jesus who must die for mankind, history (as we have observed in the prior discussion) nonetheless etches a portrait of a worried fugitive. Setting aside the Christological message that he was knowingly fulfilling God's plan, we may make the compelling surmise: Jesus had come to Jerusalem hoping to be anonymous and safe from Antipas, only to realize he had been betrayed by Judas. From any standpoint other than Christian theology, one sees his harsh reaction to the betrayal as irrefutable evidence Jesus was attempting to avoid arrest, not invite it.

Interestingly, the Gospel of John (John 13:22-13:27) deletes mention of Judas asking, "Is it me you mean?" thereby obviating any need for Jesus to label him a perjurer. My conjecture is that the Gospel resisted castigating Judas because his act furthered God's plan for Jesus to be arrested.

Although the Gospel of John enhances the scene with Christian motifs, we should take note of the unique account which says Simon signaled the disciple "Jesus loved," sitting next to him, to ask Jesus whom he suspected. The text reads: "The disciple Jesus loved was reclining next to Jesus. Simon gave him a sign, to inquire who he meant. So, leaning back, he asked, 'Who is it?'" to which Jesus supposedly responds: "the one to whom I give this piece of bread when I have dipped it." Worth noting for the purpose of this study is the presence, I propose, of Matthias, here called, "the disciple Jesus loved." Not much later when Jesus is captured and taken to the hearing before Caiaphas, we realize Matthias was indeed that very disciple—inasmuch as he has the authority of a scribe to enter the proceedings while Simon waits outside.

The reader should refer to Part I section D. which fully identifies Matthias as a scribe and details his various Gospel appearances as the friend of Jesus chosen by Simon's initiative to fill the postmortem vacancy left by Judas Iscariot.

Arrest

Retreating to the Garden of Gethsemane on the eastern side of Jerusalem, near the bottom of the Mount of Olives, Jesus' intention to avoid his captors is obvious.

As the scene unfolds (Matthew 26:37-38; Mark 14:33-35), Simon and the sons of Zebedee accompany him farther than the others, reaching a place where they then remain stationed as his personal guards. Proceeding farther, Jesus "fell prostrate on the ground and prayed (Matthew 23:39), 'Father, remove this cup from me, not because I will it (or, for my sake), but according to Your will.'" Although the image of Jesus praying resonates as a Christian symbol of his human-ness, evoking deep emotion over his readiness to die "for mankind," close scrutiny of the moment leads, once again, to a historically dissimilar assessment. In sharp contrast to the church message, the Gethsemane Jesus could not have been more intent on avoiding capture than he was at this juncture. The evidence is twofold.

First, we should inquire whether his prayer reveals a willingness to die—or is accorded that meaning by Christian belief.

In addressing God as "Father" ("abba" in the Aramaic and Hebrew), Christianity understands him to be speaking in an especially intimate and private manner, one only possible as His "son." The fact that calling God "Father" is an attested usage in Hebrew prayer, however, indicates Jesus was following a traditional form of reverent address. His other words, deferring to God's will—which therefore become Christianity's evidence of his readiness to die for the sins of mankind —are, however, also a standard expression of Hebrew faith taken directly from ancient liturgy. When, he concludes, "not because I will it/for my sake, but according to Your will" the vernacular is well-known. Jews have, since antiquity, used the same wording with only minor variation, praying: "Aveenu (our father) hosheeaynu (save us) beertzon-cha/l'mancha according to Your will."

Even his style of worship is consistent with the tradition of the day. As Matthew 26:39 states: "He fell on his face and prayed..." indicating the once customary act (Hebrew: "Ko-reem u-mishta-cha-veem") of Jews falling prostrate to engage God in heartfelt prayer.

Second, his single-minded preoccupation with avoiding capture, confirms the impression his prayer reflected no inclination to be sacrificed for mankind.

As the Gospels of Matthew and Mark describe (with some variation in Luke), Jesus ends his prayer by checking on Simon and the Zebedees only to find they have fallen asleep. He is upset at their failure to remain alert, and chastises them, saying: "The spirit is willing but the flesh is weak," and advises they pray "so you won't be tempted (to fall asleep again)."

Again retreating farther into the garden, Jesus repeats his prayer. Soon after, he makes his way to Simon and the Zebedees and once more they are asleep. Offering no excuse for their second lapse, they are reticent as Jesus retreats to pray once more.

When he returns to them a third time, they are asleep again—and the arresting party, guided by Judas, approaches.

Only because Jesus' prayer did actually occur, was it preserved in the Gospels. His terror and desperation, manifest in his repeated effort to keep Simon and the Zebedees awake, along with his grim plea to God that he be saved, could not be expurgated, but have been Christianized to exemplify self-sacrifice. Historically, Jesus had no other preoccupation than his own safety.

Finally, one may fairly inquire who it was that witnessed and reported the details concerning his prayer as well as his admonition to Simon and the Zebedees to stay awake. Based on his being with Jesus all the time (Acts 1:22), and gaining admission to the hearing before Caiaphas only a short while after his arrest, we may infer it was Matthias (See Part I D).

Given the chaos of the moment, it should not be surprising that the Gospels vary in their descriptions. In common, and believably, they record the famed "kiss" whereby Judas gave the captors a sign of which one was Jesus.

Also having the ring of authenticity, Jesus asks the arresting party, "Have you come to capture me as if I am a common thief with swords and clubs? Day after day I was with you in the Temple (courtyards) teaching and you did not arrest me" (Mark 14:48-49).

As he is being bound, and about to be led away, Jesus makes a plea in behalf of his disciples, saying, "If I am the one you are after, let these others go" (John 18:8). Acceding to his request, the captors permit them to get away. As Mark 14:50 relates: "All of them deserted him and fled."

Two of his companions apparently did not. Simon stayed close enough to be present in the vicinity of the hearing which followed

Jesus' arrest —and Matthias, having official stature as a scribe, joined the procession to Caiaphas' house, where he gained entry.

What may, on the surface, seem a narrative episode of little theological consequence, is, in fact, a seminal moment in the development of the fledgling church message. Both during the arrest, and in a subsequent quotation of Caiaphas, supposedly prior to the hearing, a sentiment is expressed which will become a cornerstone of Christian belief. Jesus' plea to his captors, "If I am the one you are after let these others go" conjoined with Caiaphas' opinion, "It is better that one man die for many, than many for one" (John 18:14) are ultimately transmuted into: "He died to save us." Evidence of the direct Christianizing of Caiaphas' comment is found in John 11:50, a passage echoing the same theme. It reads:

> "(Caiaphas said to various Jewish officials): 'You don't seem to have grasped the situation…it is better for one man to die for the People, than for the whole nation to be destroyed…' as high priest he made this prophesy, 'Jesus was to die for the nation—and not for the nation only…but for (all) the children of God.'"

What strange alchemy it is that has turned the high priest, one of the supposed main "villains" who surrenders Jesus to be executed–into a prophet speaking for God saying Jesus must die to save mankind.

Historically, the midrash is surprisingly transparent. Caiaphas, actually, was confronting a sad choice: the execution of Jesus versus the execution of Jesus along with his disciples. If he let Jesus go, he would likely be condemning them all to a bloody roundup–a concern he voices by referring to them as "all the/his people" (John 11:50).

Further enhancing the imminent judgment of Jesus, coloring the episode with messianic overtones, the imagery of the Gospel of John's sacrificed lamb is merged with the prophetic vision of Isaiah 53:4, "Ours were the sufferings he bore…on him lies a punishment that brings us peace…God burdened him with the sins of all of us…like a lamb that is led to the slaughterhouse…"

It was a nexus of ancient prophesy with his impending tragic demise such as Jesus had never imagined. Nor, at the time the arrest and crucifixion happened, would his own followers have conjured his purposeful death-for-mankind. Yet to dawn on Simon was the notion (as he came to insist), that God's chosen messianic king was to appear to be killed, but demonstrated his divinity via disappearance from his tomb and apparent resurrection.

So distraught was he that Jesus had been arrested, contradicting everything he believed, Simon denied knowing him—perhaps more than once (Matthew 26:72-74). Early on, the Jesus he knew as messiah-king seemed an illusion, vanishing before his eyes like a mirage. "I don't know who this man really is," he attested. And, at least just then, he meant it.

Of inestimable significance, Simon initially realized that the arrest proved what Jesus said was true. His spreading word he was king, as Jesus had warned, abetted the tetrarch's avowed intention to do to him what he had done to John. Antipas' determination to avenge the deprecation of his adulterous marriage, as well as to stifle incitement against his tetrarchy, was catalyzed, in large part, by Simon who had stirred up John's and Jesus' followers, exactly as Jesus feared. Although he had escaped the physical grasp of those hailing him King of the Jews at John's funeral gathering—their words of coronation laid the basis for the charge of sedition, catching him in the net of Roman law.

The hearing before Caiaphas

The array of witnesses and charges against Jesus are different in each Gospel. In his appearance before Caiaphas, the Gospel of John says only that he was "asked questions about his teaching." When he again indicates (as in Mark 14:49 at the scene of his arrest) that the guards have heard him in the Temple —and know he did or said nothing wrong —one of them slaps him in the face.

In the Gospels of Matthew and Mark witnesses come forward to charge Jesus with threatening violence to the Temple, one saying he said he could destroy it, and the other, he *would* destroy it, and in both, their testimony quotes his supposed claim to have power to rebuild it in three days. (The three-day time frame is a repetitive Christianizing component evoking his resurrection after three days in the tomb.) Neither Luke nor John make reference to such testimony. Notably, Mark 14:56 states: "Many bore false witness against him and their testimony did not agree." The Gospel of Matthew (26:60) says much the same thing.

In all four Gospels, however, only one charge is paramount—the one which will ultimately be sanctioned as a capital crime under Roman law. As we know from the inscription over the cross his offense was claiming to be King of the Jews ("Jesus of Nazareth King of the Jews").

At the hearing before Caiaphas, Jesus is asked to say whether he is or is not the messiah-king. (The word "Christ" in Matthew, Mark and Luke migrates from the Greek and Latin vernacular, but would not have been used by the high priest or traditional Jews.) In Matthew 26:64 the text reads: "(Caiaphas demanded)...tell us if you are the (messiah-king), the son of God," to which Jesus replies, "You have said it..." As discussed earlier, this formulation was a legal counter-accusation that the accuser was bearing false witness.

What was the falsehood? No other possibility exists than that the charge was he *claimed* to be King of the Jews. That was the "crime" of which he was found guilty. In that he responded to it with the legal counter-accusation of "bearing false witness," Jesus was saying he was innocent of the charge, meaning innocent of ever claiming to be King of the Jews.

Because his usage is in the day's legal vernacular, the question persists as to whether he actually denied being the messiah.

Put simply: Why didn't Jesus tell his accusers (as he had emphasized repeatedly to his disciples) "I do not claim to be, nor am I the messiah"?

[Note: Among varied examples of his earlier denials one should recall his saying to his disciples, "Why do you call me good. Only God is good!" In John 10:32-35, he rejects the idea he is claiming anything exceptional by saying he is a son of God—arguing *all* (my italics) those who have insight from God are the same and are actually called sons of god" in Psalm 82:6. No less emphatic are his continual reprimands of those—especially Simon—who reverentially address him as, "Lord." Most explicit, is his denunciation of Simon for thinking him the messiah—declaring on the road to Jerusalem, "You are walking at the side of a man—not a god!" and warning that his calling him King of the Jews may get him arrested and killed.]

Luke 22:67 supplies the reason for his reticence at the hearing. When Caiaphas demands, "Tell us if you are the messiah-king," Jesus replies: "If I tell you, you will not believe" (non-Christianized meaning: "No matter what I say, you will think I am guilty. If I tell you I have never claimed to be King of the Jews, nor thought of myself as such, you will not believe me").

The legal formulation, accusing the accuser of bearing false witness, is actually Jesus' only recourse, since, no matter what denial he made that he believed himself king, he would still have been considered guilty of fraudulently *pretending* to be king and so, seditiously misleading the Jewish populace (Luke 23:4).

Whether, in fact, he was a religious fraud—duping his naive devotees by falsely claiming to be King of the Jews—or actually believed himself to be King of the Jews, made no legal difference. Either way, he was guilty of sedition, a verdict that he could not change by testifying in his own behalf.

Reworded by the Gospel author of Mark 14:61-62, "transcending" his true plight, the revised text has Jesus substitute theology for history by affirming his divine identity, saying, "I am (King of the Jews)."

What role did Jews play in Jesus' hearing before Caiaphas?

In attempting to credibly address this most serious question, let us first mute the Gospel voice which has led to wars and hatred, separating the possible involvement of Jews from the impossible. Keeping in mind, none of Jesus' disciples—excepting Matthias—were witnesses, the varied Gospel entries, as different as they are one from the other, were altered from Matthias' original account. Still, searching for their shared theme, and his likely record of events, one is struck by the fact they have this in common: At least some of the Jews at the hearing before Caiaphas were called as witnesses. According to Jewish law, a death sentence required at least two eye-witnesses. Therefore, those claiming to have seen Jesus "stir up the People" (Luke 23:5), claiming to be a God-sent king, were legally necessary for the indictment.

Whatever else they may have testified, casting a shadow of guilt over Jesus, there was only one accusation that mattered: Two would have to say, "I saw and heard him claim to be King of the Jews."

Amazingly, according to the Gospels, none among them said so. Instead, the required eyewitnesses testified Jesus only claimed he "could/would destroy the Temple..." probably not even a crime, as unlikely as it is that he ever said such a thing about God's House, and certainly not a transgression punishable by death.

Selectively, here is how the Gospels describe the problem in getting the Jewish witnesses to provide testimony supporting a guilty verdict: **"Now (Caiaphas) sought testimony against Jesus necessary to put him to death, but could get none–and their testimony did not agree" (Matthew 26:59-60; Mark 14:55-56).**

Caiaphas, paying little heed to what else the witnesses say, since it didn't matter, tries to get Jesus to confess to the actual charge: "Tell us if you are the messiah/King of the Jews!" (Here, returning the word "Christ" to its equivalent Jewish vernacular) (Mark 14:61; Luke 22:67).

Despite the High Priest's determination to obey Torah law regarding witnesses, he failed. Frustrated, he declares, telling those who apparently demur, "It is better that only he die–than all his followers with him" (John 18:14). Ominously, the one bringing the charge–Antipas–is not mentioned at the hearing.

Aware the tetrarch is in league with Pilate (for reasons given below), and any failure to send Jesus for judgment will be considered disobedience to Rome, he does so.

The judgment before Pontius Pilate

Mocked, slapped and beaten, Jesus is led away and taken to Pontius Pilate (called "governor" or "procurator" with duties as adjudicator of capital crimes occurring in the vicinity of Jerusalem).

Portrayed by Gospel narrative as the son of God, now accepting his divinely ordained fate to die for the sins of mankind, Jesus suggests the procurator is only yielding to vengeful Jewish accusations that he claims to be King of the Jews (John 18:33-36). Pilate, confirming this supposed fact, opines, "It is your own People and priests who have handed you over to me."

When he then inquires, "(Do you say you are) King of the Jews?" Jesus supposedly reveals his divine stature, replying (selectively): "Mine is not a kingdom of this world...yes, I am a king. I was born for this..."

"So you are a king, then?" Pilate again queries, appearing mildly amused, as if he intends to fairly weigh Jesus' defense against "the many charges" (Matthew 27:14; Mark 15:4).

But having been asked about being the king a second time, Jesus employs the phraseology he used in the hearing before Caiaphas: "It is you who say it" (John 18:37 or "You have said so" Matthew 27:11). As discussed above, his usage was equivalent to saying, "You are bearing false witness against me by charging that I claim to be King of the Jews."

Next in the Gospel rendition of events according to Matthew, Mark and John, Pilate resists the vicious Jewish "priests and elders," even attempting to dissuade them from their bloodthirsty demand Jesus be crucified (Matthew 27:24-25; Mark 16:12-14; Luke 23:21-23).

(Note: Although contemporary Christian theologians, as well as the Vatican II *Nostra Aetate* declaration of 1965 "acquitted" the Jewish People of national blame for Jesus' death —millenia of emotional contempt still poison the relevant Gospel passages. As the reader may be aware, the modern Christian consensus has preserved the sanctity of the controversial passages by blaming only those Jews who bore contemporaneous responsibility–not all Jews. A meeting of the minds, with modern Jews and Christians seeking an ecumenical relationship, focuses on two points: One, crucifixion was a Roman form of punishment, proving Roman responsibility for Jesus' execution. Two, the supposed mob of priests and elders screaming "crucify him" is implausible since judicial proceedings never occurred on the first day of Passover and only the Gospel of John places the crucifixion just prior to the festival's start.)

Quite in contrast to all previous inquiries, what follows is arguably the first correct textual analysis and historical account of Jesus' judgment by Pilate.

Fortunately for history, the Gospel of Luke contains a passage which enables us to sift fact from fiction in the narrative. The text (Luke 23:6-16) describes Pilate as facing a legal issue since Jesus was a Galilean and "belonged to Antipas' jurisdiction." As a result of Jesus' place of residence, Pilate "sent him over to Antipas who was in Jerusalem at the time." Antipas is then said to have interrogated Jesus, as he and his own soldiers "treated him with contempt and mocked him, then arraying him in gorgeous apparel (a purple robe of royalty, as in Mark 15:17) sent him back to Pilate" (Luke 23:11).

If one wonders whether Jesus had been a fugitive from Antipas, the passage stating, "(Pilate) sent him over to Antipas..." leaves no doubt he was nearby waiting for him with his contingent of personal guards.

In consonance with his role as tetrarch, as we now discern, Antipas had charged, according to Roman law, that Jesus claimed to be King of the Jews. The evidence is his mocking his "kingship" by bedecking him in royal apparel and treating him with contempt.

Where were Antipas and his men actually situated? Exactly where one would expect as the guest of the procurator—in his house (the praetorium), just to the rear of the courtyard with its "seat of judgment," a paved courtyard called Gabbatha.

Fully absent the participation of Antipas, the Gospel accounts of Matthew, Mark and John do not even mention the tetrarch or suggest he was there. Instead, they vaguely imply Jesus was mocked by Pilate's own cohort.

But why, one may fairly inquire, would Pilate viciously mock Jesus, or show him contempt? Such behavior is the complete opposite of his compassionate demeanor (Matthew 27:24-25) as he only reluctantly agrees to deliver the verdict of crucifixion.

Correctly understood, the only mockery exhibited by Pilate occurred when he showed mirth at the sight of Jesus adorned by Antipas' royal robe, then fit with a crown of thorns, and forced to hold a reed scepter—before which Antipas' men bowed in feigned obeisance.

In fact, because Pontius Pilate was Rome's adjudicator of capital crimes in Jerusalem, one might have expected him to refuse Antipas' request Jesus be crucified. Given their mutual antipathy, owing to conflicting interests, that outcome would have been more likely, had it not been for an odd circumstance which inclined him toward the severe verdict.

Based on the writings of Josephus, one may surmise the following sequence and explanation: For years, Antipas and the procurator had no love for one another. Stemming from a case taken before the emperor for a decision some years earlier, they held each other in contempt. On that occasion, Antipas had protested Pilate's issuing coins with idolatrous imagery (the littus and simpulum), as well as permitting Roman soldiers to enter Jerusalem with armor bearing the emperor's image. Acting in behalf of his loyal Herodian Pietists, the tetrarch succeeded in persuading Tiberius to overrule Pilate, who was forced to stop circulating the coins or adorning the military with their graven images (Josephus; Antiquities 18:3, 56-57); a "Jewish" gesture to the Pietists for endorsing his adulterous wedlock to Herodias.

More recently, however, Pilate was apparently again summoned to the court of the emperor to defend a Samaritan complaint he had massacred many of them to establish order. If he could bring Antipas as a favorable witness, the outcome would be his complete exoneration (Josephus; Antiquities 4:1-2). In other circumstances, the tetrarch might have declined to appear in his behalf. Now, however, a new element was in the balance. Antipas wanted something in exchange for his testimony: the life of Jesus.

So it was, that sharing a laugh at the sight of the foolish-looking king, "Antipas and Pilate became friends with each other...for before this they had been enemies" (Luke 23:12).

Contrary to historical verities, the role of the Jews as depicted in the Gospels' scene of judgment before Pilate is an act of theological vandalism which begins with "Barabbas."

Intending to demean Jewish elders and priests, the Gospels all join in the invention of Barabbas, a murderer (Mark 15:6) whose release they request instead of Jesus (fulfilling the emperor's customary pardon of a criminal in honor of Passover).

Inherent in his criminal nature, Barabbas is more than just a rebel against Rome (as he is depicted in Mark 15:6 to contrast him with Jesus' followers), he is covenanted with a different power–the devil, not God. This idea is expressed in the fantasy name "Bar-Abbas," meaning "son of the father."

The concept of the "devil's son" is paralleled in John 8:41. In Jesus' retort to a group of Pietists, as they are intending to stone him for supposedly claiming to be God's son (during the Hanukkah melee), Jesus declares, "What you are doing (planning my death) is what your father (the devil, not God) does."

Just prior to the crucifixion, in its most glaring anti-Jewish polemic, the Gospels render the portrait of savage Jews preferring freedom for "one of their own," a son of the devil, rather than the son of God. Put simply, the Jews (satan's progeny) chose a son of the devil whose life they would save–over the son of God, whose death they ensured.

As tormented and twisted as Jesus on the cross, Christian scripture was dooming Jesus to die by the will of the devil's sons–the Jews.

On a technical note, this story neither exhibits the literary form of a midrash nor, strictly speaking, of a parable. For it to be a midrash (see other Gospel examples, exorcism at Kfar Nahum, Cana, "temptation" on the Jerusalem mount, the miracles of walking on water, feeding the masses, and calming the storm, and others addressed in prior discussions)–it would have to conceal a historical core. Insinuating the Jews were sons of the devil does not conform to the genre. Furthermore, unlike made-up legends that teach a spiritual lesson (the essence of a parable), the Barabbas fiction has no message, lofty or otherwise, about having faith or being righteous. It is nothing less than a malevolent slander.

Before assessing the Gospel version of the Jewish role in encouraging Jesus' crucifixion, we should keep in mind the following <u>historical</u> sequence:

1. Jesus appears before the High Priest, Caiaphas. He has been charged with claiming to be "King of the Jews," as Caiaphas has been made aware (presumably by Antipas in concurrence with Pontius Pilate) but no witnesses testify to his guilt (Matthew 29:59-60).

2. Caiaphas has been warned that if Jesus is not sent to Pilate for judgment, the rest of his entourage will be rounded up and put to death. Caiaphas therefore asserts it is best that only Jesus die, rather than all of them, and has him taken to Pilate for judgment (John 18:14).
3. Pilate hands him over to Antipas, who has been inside the procurator's house–the praetorium with his soldiers. When they emerge, Jesus is bedecked in a royal purple robe (Luke 23:11).
4. Outside, Antipas' men force him to hold a reed "scepter" and, placing a crown made of twisted thistles on his head, mockingly bow before him, saying "Hail, King of the Jews" (John 19:1-6).
5. After a few moments of shared humor, Pilate interrogates Jesus, asking if he is guilty of the charge of being "King of the Jews" (Mark 15:2).

Continuing with the non-historical Christianizing enhancements:
6. The Gospels then portray a mild-mannered Pontius Pilate doing his best to acquit Jesus. The text also suggests Antipas agreed with him that Jesus had "done nothing wrong" (Luke 23:15).
7. In a last attempt to get the bloodthirsty Jews to change their minds, Pilate offers to free Jesus in honor of Passover. The chief priests and elders choose the freedom of Barabbas, insisting on Jesus' death sentence, demanding, "Crucify him! Crucify him!"

Both Jewish and Christian studies have made the case that the portrayal of a compassionate Pilate is false. His cruelty was well-known even to the Roman rulers, who eventually banished him. Disputing the role of the supposedly vicious Jews, including "high priests" and "elders," scholars have pointed out the impossibility they would have joined such a proceeding. Rather, their religious obligations required they oversee Passover rituals in the Temple area.

Although these arguments ring true, they do not prevent Christian fundamentalists from persisting in their malignant adherence to "revealed scripture." Their one concession, as noted above, is that only *some* Jews were guilty, although they were the leaders of the People.

Critical analysis of the text, as this discussion will now show, offers undeniable proof that the Jewish involvement in the judgment by Pilate is a complete fabrication.

First, based on the analysis to this point, one may be aware the portrayal of the Jews at Caiaphas' home for a hearing is totally different in tone than the description of those Jews supposedly witnessing Pilate's judgment. In fact, despite Caiaphas' efforts to have them testify, they refuse to bear false witness and will not say that Jesus was guilty of claiming to be King of the Jews. In contrast, the Jews (as Christianized in the Gospels) who are supposedly in Pilate's Gabbatha courtyard, are venomous. Significantly, unlike those in Caiaphas' house, they do not care about Torah law requiring two eye-witnesses. Yet, they are supposedly the most observant of all religious Jews: The "high priests and elders."

The difference between the two groups of Jews is the clue to reaching a critical conclusion: Based on textual analysis, the fabricated "vicious Jews" shouting to crucify Jesus during the judgment by Pilate, are authored by the same Gospel editor who created Barabbas. In other words, when the "ruthless Jews," high priests, elders and others shout "Crucify him!" their words are in reply to Pilate offering to free Barabbas in his stead.

A critical observation concerning the Barabbas literary invention

The text of Mark 15:12-15:15 is eloquent evidence that the words "crucify him" were part of the made-up story of Barabbas:

> "Then (Pilate asked) what shall I do with the man whom you call /is called King of the Jews? And they cried out, 'Crucify him!' And Pilate said to them, 'Why? What evil has he done?' But they shouted more loudly, 'Crucify him!' So Pilate, wishing to satisfy the crowd, released for them Barabbas...and delivered Jesus to be crucified."

Surmising that Matthias was witness to the mockery of Jesus, we may conclude that he made record of Antipas' guards shouting "crucify him," as attested in John 19:6. The editorial gloss turning Antipas' cohort into Jewish devils was a theological atrocity.

Before turning to the crucifixion itself, a final related question must be addressed: Were the Pietists bloodthirsty advocates of his execution?

No. The Herodians, those Pietists who brought the report of Jesus being hailed King of the Jews from the scene of John's eulogy to Antipas, were not bloodthirsty. Their absolute refusal to testify at the Caiaphas' hearing that Jesus ever said he was the King of the Jews acquitted him of sedition according to Jewish law. Only because there was a predetermined verdict by Pilate to satisfy Antipas did Caiaphas hand him over. In other words, the Pietist Herodians acted badly in bringing their reports to the tetrarch, but ultimately refused to abet the crucifixion. Even Caiaphas, when viewed through the prism of his subservience to Rome, seems far less the embodiment of evil incarnate than he is a pathetic weakling, rationalizing a despicable decision to pander to Roman authority.

These truths were preserved in the Gospels, albeit well beneath the surface of theological enhancement and alteration, almost certainly by the actual account of Matthias, the only one of Jesus' entourage, I maintain, who was there to witness them.

The crucifixion

On the road to Golgotha, the site of crucifixion, the invented Jewish miscreants who have supposedly forsaken Passover law to demand Jesus' death, simply aren't there. If they had been, the Gospels would have certainly said so.

In fact, because there are no Jews along the route, the soldiers force Simon, a Cyrene, "on his way into the city from the country" to lift one end of the cross (Mark 15:21). John 19:17 says Jesus carried it by himself, though this seems less likely. Filling the streets, empty due to the Temple Passover ceremonies, Luke alone states "following after him was a great multitude of the people and of women who bewailed him..."

Once there, the ghastly Roman form of execution is recorded without much detail. Just prior to his being nailed to the cross (though this gruesome event is not described), Jesus is offered a palliative of wine mixed with myrrh, which he turns down (Mark 15:23).

Then a sign reading, "Jesus of Nazareth King of the Jews" is affixed to the top of the vertical wooden beam where it would be visible overhead. Regarding the inscription, the Gospel of John says that it was rendered in three languages, Hebrew, Latin and Greek (John 19:21) though Mark says only that it read "King of the Jews" (Mark 15:26) paralleling a variation in Matthew (27:37) "This is Jesus King of the Jews," with Luke making no mention of a sign or inscription whatsoever. Christian tradition has imagined the inscription to be an abbreviation of the Latin, "INRI."

According to the narrative of Mark, the time was the "third hour" or nine in the morning when Jesus was crucified (Mark 15:25). Again according to Mark (15:27 paralleled by Matthew 27:38), to Jesus' right and left were two robbers. Only after six hours of agony (Mark 15:34), is Jesus reported to have spoken.

With his life ebbing, his voice is so parched that a vinegar-soaked sponge must be held on a stick for him to wet his mouth, enabling him to be understood.

According to the narrative, his words, "Eli, Eli lama sabachthani" were barely audible. Though "Eli" means "my God," there was reportedly a question as to whether he hadn't actually said, "Eliyahu," meaning Elijah, as if there were Jews present to recognize such a possibility. Textually the inference Jews were at the crucifixion should be dismissed as a thematic echo of the Barabbas composition, with the priests and elders suddenly on hand to taunt Jesus to save himself, or have Elijah do it, and prove he is the son of God (Matthew 27:41-43;27:49 Mark 15:31-32; Mark 15:36. Notably, Luke and John have no similar account).

Before considering the actual translation of "Eli, Eli lama sabachthani," we should take note of two unique passages in John. The first is the sole record that as Jesus was dying, the soldiers divided up his clothing among four of them. Even his underwear went to one who won it with a toss of dice (John 19:23-19:24).

The second (John 19:25) is a remarkable quote of a fully audible Jesus speaking to his mother whose presence at the crucifixion is mentioned only here. As he sees her standing at the side of (Matthias) "the disciple Jesus loved," Jesus says: "...Woman, this is your son." Then to Matthias ("the disciple"), "This is your mother," to which the narration adds: "And from that moment he made a place for her in his home."

Simultaneously, introduced by the Gospel of John as witnesses "near the cross" are: Mary the wife of Cleopas and Mary Magdala, unlike the other Gospels, which say the two Marys "watched from afar" (Mary Magdalene and Mary the wife of Cleopas are called variously Mary, the mother of James the younger, mother of the Zebedees, or of Jose, and Salome in Matthew 27:56; Mark 15:40).

Given that Jesus' mother is glaringly absent from all related passages referring to bystanders, and occurs in no other Gospel crucifixion scene, how may one explain her interposition in the Gospel of John? Linguistic analysis supplies the answer.

According to the wording of Jesus' supposed instruction from the cross, he tells Mary, "*Woman*, this is your son" and to (Matthias), "she is your mother." His meaning, as the Gospel indicates, is that Mary be "taken care of"– rendered as: "From that moment (Matthias) made a place for her in his home."

A critical reconstruction recognizes an altogether different scenario. Hypothetically, the correct Greek original, instead of "gune" meaning "woman" was "gumnos" meaning "nakedness." Substituting "nakedness" for "woman" in John 19:26, we may retrieve the following. Jesus spoke from the cross to the disciple I have identified as Matthias, saying:

"Take care of my nakedness."

Supporting this assessment, one should note its perfect fit in the context and sequence of events. Whether the soldiers did, or did not, actually divide his clothing among themselves, the Gospel text indicating they did –and that Jesus was therefore naked –directly precedes the instruction to Matthias to "take care of my nakedness."

Furthermore, not long after Jesus is taken down from the cross, John states (19:40): "The body of Jesus was wrapped...in linen cloth, according to Jewish burial custom."

(Note: The non-historical "presence" of Jesus' mother at the cross may have found a place in John as a motif useful in winning converts among Egyptians and followers of the northern syncretistic theologies. They would better appreciate the "fallen savior" if modelled after Isis and Horus as depicted in their iconography, which becomes the Christian "pieta." It is also quite likely, though conjectural, that Matthias did actually show postmortem concern and hospitality to a grieving Mary, which may have inspired the misquote of Jesus on the cross.)

Because much of Jesus' final travail appears to be drawn from Psalm 22, the reader is advised that various elements of the Gospel scene are conjectural.

Here are examples of descriptive elements in the psalm, suggesting Jesus' fate was preordained by Hebrew scripture—and which, therefore, may be the source of textual midrashic enhancements.

1. Deriding voices, say "let's see his God save him now" (Matthew 27:43 from Psalm 22 line 9. Psalm 42:4 also reflects this sentiment).
2. "I am poured out like water and all my bones are out of joint" (Psalm 22 line 15, compare this to John 19:34).
3. "My tongue cleaves to my throat" (Psalm 22 line 16, compared to Jesus' parched words).
4. "They split my garments among them and cast lots for them" (John 19:24; also Luke 23:34 from Psalm 22 line 19).

Returning to the last moments of Jesus' life as he was expiring, his instruction to Matthias/aka "the disciple" that he take care of his nakedness (with a linen shroud), is followed by his barely audible words: "Eli, Eli lama sabachthani."

Standard translations read this as: "My God, My God, why have you forsaken me?"

But did Jesus actually cry out, "Eli, Eli lama sabachthani"? Arguably, he did. Again taking note of Psalm 22, which seems to be a possible source for the lament, we encounter different wording—with the psalmist asking God, "Lama *azavtani.*" "Azavtani" indeed means "forsaken me," but "sabachthani" with the root being s-v-ch, does not. This root, as it occurs in the Gospel itself, rather than replicating the psalm, is better rendered: "Why have you killed/destroyed me?"

It is a translation which differs from "Why have you forsaken me?" not only in tone but in substance. Arguably, the Christianizing of "Why have you killed/destroyed me?" faces a theological conundrum. If Jesus is blaming God, lamenting, "Why have you killed/destroyed me?" how will he be a model for mankind, overcoming suffering through faith in heavenly salvation?

In contrast to his expression of ignorance, asking why God is punishing him with death ("lama sabachthani," an ignorance incompatible with his messianic omniscience), the Psalmist's prayerful, "lama azavtani/Why have you forsaken me?" (as usually adapted to and translated into the Gospel English) is a more resonant Christian symbol of Jesus' purpose on earth. Indeed, "lama azavtani" (Psalm 22) are words echoing mankind's need to feel God's loving Presence even at the moment of expiring. But, because Matthias recorded what Jesus had actually said, "Lama sabachthani? Why have you killed me!" the disciples dared not change them. The fact most English versions of the Gospels have distorted their translation strongly suggests Jesus' actual words on the cross were impossible to reconcile with faith in his messiahship.

At the end of his life, Jesus' last words, according to the Gospel of John, were, "It is accomplished" (John 19:30).

Perhaps months later, as his disciples struggled to understand why God had "destroyed" Jesus, the Greek vernacular, "teleio"–meaning, "accomplished/fulfilled/made perfect" was accepted as their cognate for whatever Aramaic vocabulary he had actually uttered. Certainly, their initial reaction to his crucifixion was that they had been wrong –that he could not have been the messiah king. That, after all, was the same as Simon's reaction when, on the way from Caesaria Philipi, Jesus warned him he would be arrested if the talk he was king persisted: "Lord, this shall not (or, cannot) happen to you!" Simon had protested (Matthew 16:22).

Only if Jesus had an intentional plan to be arrested and murdered, would Simon and the others be fully acquitted of abetting his demise.

Their insights into Jesus' "secret" divine agenda thus became the "stuff" of Christianity—saving their king from true death (being resurrected) and, in the process saving themselves from confessing even to themselves what they had done.

That Jesus is required by Christian theology to say, "It is accomplished," breathing his last, as he frees his followers from any responsibility for his death, must stand out as an affront to the historical Jesus matched only by the crucifixion itself.

Echoed in Matthew 5:18, when Jesus is reputed to declare Torah will be passe once "all is accomplished," the Gospel coverup becomes a requiem for the historical Jesus, and a thematic interment of everything he believed.

But what were his last words?

Most likely addressing Matthias, his beloved friend who remained with him through his agony, he would have him hear the end of his inhuman misery was occurring.

Without adornment, he would simply have gasped, "It is (or, "I am") finished."

Entombment, disappearance

The Gospels report the events as follows:

Jesus' body was "taken down" from the cross (Mark 15:46; Luke 23:53), or, was "taken/taken away" (Matthew 27:59; John 19:38) by a man named Joseph of Arimathea (a "rich man" Matthew 27:57; "a respected member of the council /Sanhedrin" Mark 15:43, Luke 23:50; "a secret disciple" John 19:38).

Pilate gave permission to take the body (all four Gospels).

Joseph wrapped Jesus' body in a new linen shroud and laid it in "his own new tomb" (Matthew 27:60) or, "in a tomb which had been hewn out of rock" (Mark 15:46, Luke 23:53) or, in "a new tomb in a nearby garden" (John 19:41).

Here are the unique and significant details in John's account of the body's removal (selectively, John 19:38-41):

"Nicodemus, who had at first come to Jesus by night, also came bringing a mixture of myrrh and aloes, weighing about a hundred pounds. They (that is, Nicodemus and Joseph of Arimathea) took the body of Jesus and wrapped it with spices in linen cloths, according to the burial custom of the Jews."

The reference to Nicodemus who came to Jesus "at night" is found in John 3:1, saying he was "a leading Jew." In a conversation with Jesus on an earlier occasion, Nicodemus supposedly asks Christianized questions about being "reborn," which Jesus explains in a doctrinal sermon about "the spirit" and rebirth through water, "the baptism."

The importance of this prior appearance of Nicodemus is its textual context, which places it in the timeframe of a Passover occurring at least a year before the fateful festival when he was arrested. During this "first" Passover, John describes Jesus' supposed turning over the tables of the money changers—an event which, according to the other Gospels (Matthew 21:12; Mark 11:15) took place the day before his last meal and arrest. Therefore, it is reasonable to hypothesize there was actually only one attested Passover episode, and no historical, earlier Passover when Nicodemus encountered Jesus. Merging the two Passovers described in John into one (as in the other Gospels) we are left with a single, important piece of information about Nicodemus: *He came twice, first, at night, not with Joseph of Arimathea, but to assist Matthias in doing what Jesus had asked, taking Jesus' body away from the cross, and wrapping him in a shroud and again, this second time with Joseph "of Arimathea" after the Shabbat was over.*

Based on this supposition, we should posit the following question:

If Nicodemus came first at night (that is just as the sun was setting and the Shabbat was about to begin), and, if he didn't return with Joseph of Arimathea to salve him with myrrh and aloes until Saturday ended after sunset, or even in the pre-dawn hours of Sunday, where had Matthias and Nicodemus left Jesus' body for those preceding 24-34 hours?

Pending removal for final interment, either to a common public graveyard–such as was the "Aceldama" located in the Valley of Hinnom, or, by a family member to a private tomb, they would have placed Jesus in a nearby cave which served as a temporary repository for the remains of those who were crucified.

Further complicating the actual sequence of events, are the Gospel variations concerning the disposition of the body. In Mark and Luke the burial spices were brought to the tomb a day after Jesus had been placed in it, that is, after the Shabbat on Sunday morning (Mark 16:2; Matthew 28:1; Luke 24:1). But it was not Nicodemus who did so (though he is said to have done so in John 19:38-41, quoted above). Rather, it was Mary Magdalene and another "Mary, the mother of James." Mark adds a third woman, Salome, whereas in Luke 23:55 they are simply called "the women who had followed him from the Galilee." Nor do they ever put the spices on the body because it was gone from the tomb by the time they arrived.

Moreover, in John 20:6 it was not the Marys who enter the tomb to look around, but Simon and "the disciple Jesus loved" (Matthias) who find the linen shroud where the body had been.

Finally, before putting the pieces of the puzzle together, the role of Joseph of Arimathea explicated by all four Gospels is critical. In each, Joseph goes to Pilate and asks for permission to remove the body. Mark and Luke both say Joseph then went and "took him down," somehow managing to lower and remove him. Only John adds Nicodemus as a companion of Joseph of Arimathea in retrieving the body–but does not use the wording "took him down," instead stating, "they came and took it away."

Reconstructing what actually happened

It was nearing sundown, concluding the first day of Passover, with Shabbat about to begin, a time when Jewish law prohibited burial. Matthias was joined by Nicodemus, his "first" appearance, accompanying the body to the cave used by the Romans as a temporary repository. There, fulfilling Jesus' request to "take care of my nakedness" (in conformity with Torah law), they wrapped him in a shroud and departed.

Joseph of Arimathea, variously labelled a secret disciple, or a rich man, was, as the Gospels of Mark and Luke agree, a member of the Sanhedrin ("the Council"). He requested and received permission from Pontius Pilate to take the body–which was located in the temporary cave-tomb. Because it was Shabbat, he would wait until Saturday at sundown, or the following hours to do as he had asked, and retrieve it for proper interment.

Once the Shabbat was over, as the Gospel of Matthew (27:59) relates, "Joseph...wrapped Jesus in a *clean* linen shroud" (my italics), as compared to the bloody one, which they left behind, which is echoed by John 19:38-41 (with wording re-arranged for clarity):

> "So they (Joseph of Arimathea and Nicodemus) came and...wrapped him with spices, myrrh and aloes in linen cloths according to Jewish burial customs and took (his body) away (*from the temporary cave-tomb;* my reconstruction) and according to (Matthew 27:60): "laid it in his own new tomb."

Whether "new tomb" means it was one never before used (as indicated in John 19:41) or meant "a different tomb from the first," does not alter the implication. Either way, the words: "his own new tomb" (Matthew 27:60) reveal the Gospel account is referring to one owned by Joseph of Arimathea–and provided by him for the final interment of Jesus.

Who was Joseph of Arimathea?

Reference to Jesus' nominal (if not biological) father, Joseph, in very early Christian literature (*Protoevangelium of James*) states he was a member of the Sanhedrin, the Hebrew legislative body governing civil and religious law. And this description matches his circumstances. A betrothal to his deceased wife's niece, Mary, when she was only sixteen years old, strongly suggests there was a financial component making it a desirable arrangement. His having two homes, one in Nazareth and the other in the area of Bethlehem, further supplies a portrait of a successful man.

Further, my linguistic analysis of the name "Joseph of Arimathea" and the role he plays in the Gospels (Matthew 27:57–59; Mark 15:42–46; Luke 23:50–56; John 19:38) is significant. Portrayed as a secret disciple of Jesus, he makes his only appearance following the crucifixion and helps transport Jesus' body to a "new" tomb. (According to the Gospel account, this was the only tomb to which the body was ever taken.)

Various translations of Arimathea have been suggested by scholars. Some have seen the name as a cognate for "Ram" meaning "Heights" and so could have indicated he was from the ancient city of Ramallah, or from the village just north of Jerusalem, "Ramah," made famous by the words of Jeremiah referring to Jews being gathered there on the way to Babylonian exile.

My translation, the first such, asserts it was an Aramaized mis-pronunciation of the Hebrew: Ir Ha-mayteem–literally city of the dead. The Greek equivalent –necropolis –makes my linguistic assessment compelling.

According to Roman legalities, the body could only be released for private burial to a family member who had received permission to take it from the public tomb. So, Joseph of Arimathea was, in all probability, Jesus' presumptive (non-biological) father. Naturally, he did not live in a cemetery. Therefore to say the man at the crucifixion was "Joseph from the City of the Dead" does not mean he was from a cemetery, but that he lived in its vicinity, or was a familiar visitor to his family tomb. Very possibly, those who recognized him included neighbors who would greet him on the memorial occasions typical of Jewish tradition. If so, "Arimathea" could have been attached as a pseudo-surname by them.

While it remains educated conjecture that Joseph of Arimathea was Jesus' presumed father, and that he took him for entombment to "Arimathea/Ir ha-mayteem," the necropolis near his home, it does seem unlikely Roman policy would have permitted removal of the body from the public tomb by a non-family member, or to a so-called "secret follower," who was mentioned once and only once in each of the four canonized Gospels.

Clearly, Nicodemus did not have the same connection to Jesus as did Joseph. Though he had come to the cross and joined the "disciple" (Matthias) as he took Jesus to the temporary, public cave-tomb, he was not the one to request the body. Nor did he have Joseph's stature as a member of the Sanhedrin.

Not mentioned in the other Gospels, Nicodemus' role, as one may sense, befits Joseph's servant. After all, he was a partner in the effort to bring a large and heavy amount of myrrh and aloes, wrapping Jesus in a clean shroud, and as John 19:40 indicates, then helped "remove the body and take it to a new tomb..."

Finally, one may wonder why Joseph should have cared enough about Jesus to become involved with his burial. Even more problematic, if he had such sentiments, why did he do nothing to appeal to Caiaphas or Pilate for his life which might have carried weight given his civic stature.

Though we have no concrete evidence, various explanations are plausible. Until the "disciple" (Matthias) got word to him that Jesus was dead, Joseph simply may not have known about the unfolding drama of his arrest and judgment. By the time Nicodemus would reach the area where Pilate delivered his verdict, it was too late to reverse the course of events. Or, if word spread that he had been crucified, and Nicodemus hearing gossip, hurried to Golgotha, Joseph's presence may have been delayed.

Still, he cared enough to recover the body with Nicodemus' help and take Jesus for interment to the family tomb in Ir ha-mayteem (Arimathea).

Given that he had distanced himself from Jesus after raising him until the age of twelve, one may legitimately be surprised that he still felt a familial bond. After all, nearly thirty years had passed since he had betrothed Mary and been devastated by her pregnancy. However, as her non-blood uncle, faced with a widower's obligation to secure the family holdings, a strong Jewish tradition, he chose to provide her a comfortable setting in his Nazareth home, a scandal-free environment, where Jesus would be nurtured in the company of his siblings, Joseph's offspring from the prior marriage.

There, one may assume Jesus came to know Joseph as his father, owing to his frequent visits to his other children, and his desire to play the husband/father preventing scurrilous gossip. During the later part of those twelve years, a reasonable inference is that he taught Jesus much about Jewish law and custom, perhaps introducing him to carpentry or woodworking so he would have a vocation.

When Joseph stopped coming north, perhaps spending his time in meetings of the Sanhedrin, very likely busy with his work as a builder, Jesus may have resented the separation. But from Joseph's standpoint, he had spared the family any hint of scandal over Mary's adultery and Jesus' lineage. Furthermore, he had seen to Jesus' entry into the Hebrew community by taking him to the Temple at the age of twelve for his induction into the society as an adult. (The display of Torah knowledge was a proto-Bar-Mitzvah event.)

Though it is pure conjecture, one may suspect Joseph's primary residence in the area of Bethlehem felt free from the sadness of Nazareth where Mary's indiscretion was always in the air, and Jesus, a boy he apparently loved, was a son that was not really his.

Concluding Observations

As I close the curtain on this study, the story of Jesus' life portrayed throughout has indeed seemed to take the form of a play, with each of four main acts leading fatefully to the next.

The first began with Jesus teaching his disciples Torah and showing them how to pray and give charity according to the Rosh ha-shannah tradition. About the same time, there were conflicts about healing on the Shabbat, followed by mutual recrimination—and a question of whether he wasn't claiming to heal afflictions usually considered possible signs of divine punishment. If so, Jesus was acting as though he had God's authority to forgive sin. When he mistakenly thought the screaming man in Kfar Nahum was possessed, and by touching him (as an intended exorcism) caused him to collapse, actually seized with terror, word spread Jesus was crazy and possibly evil.

Act Two, to call it that, began with the Wedding at Cana, when Jesus learned Joseph was not his biological father. (See above for complete analysis and reconstruction.) Already regarded by the community–and even his own family–as acting "crazy," especially because many uneducated locals sought his healing and teaching (also hoping to be part of God's Kingdom), Jesus now worried that his "lessons" to followers had been unintentionally winning him their devotion as God's anointed messiah king. Because he was born from Mary's adultery–as he now realized –and perhaps from the seed of a foreigner or idolator, he believed he might have been doing satan's work without even knowing it.

His great distress was the actual cause of the contemplated suicide known in Christianity as the Temptation on the Temple mount. (See analysis and reconstruction, above.) This episode occurred during the Feast of Booths in the year 31CE.

Act Two, as I am calling it, ends with Jesus choosing lineage purification by his cousin John's immersion, later known to Christianity as a baptism ceremony.

As the curtain opened on early winter, about the time Jesus was nearly stoned in the Temple courtyards during Hanukkah for supposedly exalting himself as *the* son of God (which he dismissed as a generic term found in the psalms), John was arrested. However, after the lineage-purification immersion, Jesus had changed, carefully monitoring the impression he gave others. So guarded were his words and teachings, they no longer lent themselves to any misinterpretation or suggestion that he claimed to be a divine emissary.

Just as striking, he did no more healings, thus preventing his activity from being misconstrued as forgiving sin. The only one he did do was forced on him when a paralytic man was lowered through a broken open roof, despite the fact he refused to let the afflicted individual enter through the door. And, in that instance, no cure occurred. (See reconstruction, above.)

Further, he emphasized in the strongest terms the eternal sanctity of the Torah and its every word declaring nothing in it should ever be changed until the end of time. Despite his best efforts, by midwinter teaching only in parables to insure his words could not be twisted into falsehoods, the three lakeside villages, Kfar Nahum, Chorazin and Beit Zaida banished him from entering their precincts. As a result, he told his disciples to go their own way.

During that time, when John was arrested, and up until the early spring when John was executed, Jesus (having been banished from the three towns) spent much of his time in retreat (presumably with Matthias, in his home) separated from his students, a period which Christianity later labeled "The sending away of the twelve."

The final, historically tragic act, began with Jesus' eulogy to John—first recognized and recovered in this study. When he spoke words accusing the tetrarch and his wife of an adulterous marriage, Jesus had committed the exact insult for which Herod Antipas had John arrested and executed.

As observed earlier, Jesus' words rejecting Antipas' marriage to Herodias, implying she was an adulteress, was an act of immeasurable courage. It gave voice to John who could no longer speak—but whom Jesus would never forget had stood up for him as a witness before God, in the lineage-purification ritual, his immersion.

Hailed "King of the Jews" by John's grieving throng of "lost sheep without a shepherd," Jesus "coronation" was the basis for a charge of sedition and thus he became a fugitive. In sum, unintended as it was, the disciples' adoration of Jesus had led to the legally viable capital charge, crossing political lines, and ultimately to his murder on the cross.

Although the Jerusalem locale seemed a relatively safe environment, Antipas, whose true intent was to avenge the honor of his wife, would call in a favor of its ruthless procurator, Pontius Pilate leading to the sequence of events described in this documented biography.

As a sad epitaph of the luminous young teacher, I offer a disheartening reflection:

Echoed in Matthew 5:18, Christianizing words have him declare Torah would be passe once "all is accomplished," while Jesus' last gasp on the cross in John 19:30 reverberates, "it is accomplished." With these fabricated utterances, the Gospel coverup becomes a requiem for the historical Jesus, and a thematic interment of everything he believed.

His devotees had ignored his reprimands of their misguided exaltation and, in the aftermath of his crucifixion, rather than confess having unintentionally abetted his execution, declared he was still alive in heaven. The majority of disciples and apostles of Christianity, from its theological inception shortly after the crucifixion, had concealed the historical Jesus in order to promote a salvation theology–saving themselves from the unbearable truth: they fostered the circumstances which ultimately brought about the death of the one they hailed as king–the one they believed would assure their elite roles in God's imminent Kingdom.

Disguising themselves in the nascent doctrine of Christianity, those coronating Jesus, "King of the Jews," chief among them Simon, thus spared themselves the truth of what they had done perhaps as much in their own hearts as in the forum of public awareness. They had abetted the murder of their beloved, remarkable teacher, one they believed God had sent to save them; one who should never have died for them or anybody else.

But I would not end with what others did wrong–rather with the courage Jesus showed, truly an example to us all. When he chose to speak out against a woman divorcing her husband at John's memorial gathering, echoing John's fateful criticism of Herodias for her incestuous and adulterous wedlock to Antipas–we bear witness to Jesus' true character. He would not let the cousin who had spoken up for him– fostering a restored lineage and Covenantal purification–be a voice silenced. As John had vouchsafed God's love for Jesus, Jesus now loudly sounded his beloved cousin's fateful rebuke of Antipas. It was a decision that he knew could cost him his life, and it did.

Not that his courage to speak out for what he believed should surprise us. Jesus' teaching students who were fully ignorant of Jewish religious culture, those considered to be of doubtful Hebrew lineage, was bold, if not brash, in that era.

Demonstrably, he recognized a likelihood his intentions could be misunderstood, repeatedly stating his goal was to restore to the Hebrew community followers whose ignorance had caused their appreciation of the Covenant to become frayed and forgotten.

Among his disciples several may well have felt a renewed appreciation of their ancient Covenant, returning to observance of Torah law and tradition as he taught and urged. But the majority, under Simon's sway, did not, rather seeking a different path to redemption, especially after his death. The consequence of the crucifixion itself, a violent interruption of Jesus' teaching, was catastrophic to the goals he sought. The fledgling church, with the aid of its arch theological alchemist, Paul, soon turned his gruesome demise into God's plan—not for Covenantal restoration of doubtful Hebrews—but for the inauguration of his heavenly dominion as eternal savior of mankind.

One may appropriately conclude with this final question: Was Jesus a universalist?

As a Jew, he absolutely was. The Torah and the prophets envision all mankind as fully equal before God. The ruach ha-kodesh, the holy spirit, in Jewish tradition and Torah, is the "great equalizer" giving all people the same potential to find fulfillment and inherit the blessings of life. But as a Torah-observant Jew, Jesus would never have abdicated his heritage and history in order to attract gentile proselytes, nor would he have "universalized"the supposedly provincial Jewish religion as a prelude to any other belief system's program of salvation.

Four years after his death, Antipas and Caiaphas and Pontius Pilate were banished by Rome.

Maybe God was watching.

PART THREE
APPENDICES

A. Judaism of the period –antecedents and tradition
B. Historical sequence of events critical to Jesus' last year
C. Postmortem parables

A. JUDAISM OF THE PERIOD–ANTECEDENTS AND TRADITION

THE COVENANT AND THE RELATIONSHIP WITH GOD

To grasp the Pietists' challenge to the Covenantal legitimacy of Jesus' group we must delve more deeply into the underlying concepts that shaped first century Judaism.

The inquiry begins with the antecedent eras which were formative to the relationship between the People and God. Unlike any other religion, God and the People had a bond characterized by two differing metaphors. One pictured God as the "Father" of creation, exercising a paternal guidance of Hebrew destiny–and the second, far more resonant as a source of inspiration, saw the relationship as a *spiritual marriage*. On one side, represented as the author of existence, the Creator provided a verbal marriage contract (Heb: *Ketubah*) containing a three-fold oath (the "Covenant") to: 1. protect and keep the People secure 2. to assure fecundity of both land and individuals and 3. to provide a land for the populous nation.

(Here I should note that because the Covenant was thus rooted in the concept of a matrimonial bond, it may seem completely literal–namely that the People were actually married to God. Such a view would misunderstand the poetic weight of the metaphor. It engaged the

People as it did because it enabled them to relate to God in an intimate, personal manner.)

Early in the second millenium, God set forth this Covenantal "wedding" vow to Abraham (Gen. 12:1-7, 15:1, 15:17-15:18,16:10 to Sarah, 17:1-2, 17:7, 17:9-16). Accepting the "proposal," Abraham in return, as "father of the People" (his name in Hebrew: Av=father; am=People), would "Walk in My (i.e. God's) ways and be blameless." This condition symbolically stipulated the purity expected of a bride.

Also explicated in this context, God decreed circumcision to be an absolute necessity as a sign of the bond between Him and the People (Gen: 17:9-14). Though the ritual has baffled scholars and theologians, we may now appreciate its meaning. Circumcision was actually a component in the sequence intended to define the marital relationship. First, the Covenantal vow was made, then a year of betrothal passed (Gen. 18:10), and finally the eight-day "wedding ceremony" reaching its fruition with the proof of virginity–the Bridal People shedding the blood that is typical of virgins, from the sexual organ. As a spiritual marriage, the male gender of the circumcised individual was not considered a contradiction.

About five hundred years later, in the time of Moses, the espousal of the Hebrew People by God would become even more obvious.

As recipients of the "Covenant" (Heb: *Brit*), the national "Bride" accepted and swore to keep God's statutes as stated in the marriage contract's documented form, the Ten Commandments.

The first two Commandments are specific concerning the relationship:

1. I am God–and you shall have no other. (A demand for acceptance of God by the Bridal People, and her fidelity).

2. You shall not bow down before other "gods." (The marriage was to be monogamous).

Though the demand for fidelity seems to be echoed in the second Commandment it was more a pronouncement banning any ritual participation in non-Hebrew cult practices.

That this is a statement of the wedding vow becomes increasingly clear in Exodus 19:5-6 (God says): "If you will keep my Covenant, you shall be my Holy Nation, a Kingdom of Priests."

(This sentiment, that the bride will be holy to the husband, finds its expression in the traditional wedding vow between a Jewish groom and his betrothed. Hebrew: "Haray at mikudeshet li"; literally, "With this vow, you are made holy to me.")

Responding to God's Covenantal wedding oath, the People answered: (Exodus 24:7-8) "All that God has said, we will do and pay heed to."

In Exodus 25:1 God asks that a dowery be presented [Hebrew: "Terumah," literally, "Donations," such as gold and silver, precious yarns and gems, which are to adorn the travelling desert Temple (Heb:Mishkan"). It is the "home," symbolically, that is provided by the "husband"].

Therefore, God speaks, saying (Exodus 29:43): "(The Temple tent) shall be made holy by my Presence."

Representing the Bride in the wedding ceremony, Aaron and his sons are specially dressed for the Covenantal acceptance ceremony (Exodus 29:5-12).

Of utmost importance was the purity of the Temple "Home"–and purity of the Bridal People. Therefore, Moses reported God's words (Exodus 30:17-18; 19:10 and 19:14) instructing the People to: "Make a basin of copper for washing between the entrance and the altar (that is, God's Presence) adding, "They must wash their clothes." Further (Exodus 30:17-21), the necessary washing is explicit, "...when the (priests) enter the Temple tent...they shall wash their hands and feet so they do not die."

In Moses' era, the spiritual marriage, would, as it had in the prior time of Abraham, emphasize circumcision as a component of the ceremonial commitment.

In Exodus 4:25-26, Moses' wife Zipporah circumcises their second son, Eliezer, performing a ritual of touching the foreskin to her leg and reciting an oath: "You (meaning God) are herewith my bridegroom of blood." (Both the ritual of leg-touching and the verbal formula are unattested except on that occasion). See also Exodus 12:48-51 regarding circumcision as a condition of Covenantal inclusion in the period of Moses.

Finally, the threefold wedding/Covenantal vow is dramatically rendered in the form of the Hebrew festivals, Passover (the Hebrews leaving Egypt as a bride leaves her parental environment), Shavu'ot (receiving the marriage contract, the Ten Commandments), and Sukkot (moving into dwellings built to represent the family dwellings made holy by the Presence of God). To the reader unfamiliar with the latter, Jewish tradition requires families build hut-like shelters out of doors with open-branched roofs, a holiday usually occurring in early October (the 15th of Tishrei).

In Jesus' time, as noted above, the belief God would return to the midst of the People motivated the Pietists to constantly purify their homes awaiting the "Day of God." Because no such Torah commandment existed, except pertaining to Passover, Pietists were, as Jesus' perceived them, exaggerating and imposing their beliefs concerning cleanliness on others. Also, the Sukkot dwellings which were to house God's Presence further led the Pietists to exaggerate household purity laws formerly applicable only to the Jerusalem Temple precincts. Still, the Pietists' inflated view of their own stature, was a seed planted in Moses' time, more than a millenium before Jesus.

The concept of a "Nation of Priests" was taken literally when God spoke to Moses. On Passover, the reality was made manifest as all the People cleaned their household environments to the level of purity of the Temple and offered their sacrifices. This was done without the official priests performing the ritual so that the People might be equal to the priests before God.

Adding to the established marital-metaphor manifest in the festivals, the wedding ceremony itself preceded God's moving into the Sukkot dwellings. Such was the significance of Rosh Ha-shannah (only later the Jewish New Year) which commenced the joyous wedding (ten days before Yom Kippur, and fifteen days before Sukkot). Soon after Rosh Ha-Shannah all the population became contemplative as Yom Kippur, the day of examining the Bridal People's purity–her body and heart –approached. In spirit, the wedding "procession" actually started eight days after Rosh-Ha-shannah with the ending (or test) of virginity (circumcision is always on the eighth day) and was completed three days later (Exodus 19:11) of which God said, "Let them be ready for the third day..." occurring at the end of the sacred Day of Atonement. Five days after Yom Kippur, the wedding was consummated as God's Presence entered the hut-like dwellings of Sukkot. Rainfall and fecundity were the natural consequence of the spiritual union.

Such remarkable intimacy between God and the People was achieved by contact with the Divine or holy spirit. Though Christianity has emphasized the "holy spirit" as if it were an original Christian theological doctrine, it forms the basis of the Jewish relationship with God from the very beginning of Genesis, the first book of the Torah, as discussed in an earlier part of this study.

Punishment of Infidelity (the sin of loving other gods)

As a consequence of the "spiritual marriage" motif permeating Hebrew belief from Moses' era on, terrible suffering of the People was attributed to infidelity (loving other gods)–or otherwise defiling the relationship with God through sin.

The punishment of the People, when she strayed after other gods/"lovers" was, according to the prophets, separation (national exile) and the threat of complete divorce. (As examples, see Hosea 2:8-11; Jeremiah 3:6-9.) The offense was referred to variously as "whoring" and "adultery." (Hebrew: Nee-oof)

Individuals (as well as the nation) were also responsible for keeping the Commandments. If a man or woman was proved guilty of fornication by the testimony of at least two eye witnesses, the sentence was death by stoning. (In actuality, this probably never occurred since witnesses were unlikely. The adulterous woman brought before Jesus for judgment, while exemplifying his compassion, has a different theme, and very plausibly portrays Jesus forgiving his own mother for giving birth to him from an unknown father. See prior discussion.)

Progeny of prohibited unions (to foreign enemies, or by incest, or adultery) were punishable by decree from God–a phenomenon that was thought to explain various diseases and afflictions of seemingly innocent individuals.

Among notable examples, King David's first child, it was believed, died as punishment by God for his adultery with Batsheva, and the prophet Hosea's doubtful children were given the label of foreigners, an example of "individual exile" from the community.

Defilement through infidelity of the People to God, is, naturally, different than actual sexual infidelity which occurs when a spouse is unfaithful. On the national level, the People were able eventually to return to the Covenantal fold. They did so through penance and a renewed appreciation of God–both of His power and His blessings.

Such an "appreciation" was reflected in observance of the Commandments, especially those which demonstrated a reverence for the Creator. Tithes of produce donated to the Temple, providing animals for priestly sacrifices, attendance at the Jerusalem Temple during the festivals, worship in local synagogues, studying Torah, and most important, keeping the Commandment to rest on Shabbat were signs of "appreciation" of God, the spiritual "spouse."

Lack of appreciation, or revilement of Judaism's commandments and rituals might be atoned. Still, if there was lineage-defilement and individuals were suspected of foreign or sinful histories, return to the Covenantal fold could only be offered by God. Even the suspicion that local northerners such as Jesus' followers were in that category would cause the Pietists to exclude them from interacting socially. Because people afflicted with leprosy, blindness, deafness, lameness, or madness (considered demonic possession) were thought of as possibly punished for ancestral lineage-defilement, a charismatic young teacher like Jesus, performing healings on them would have seemed to claim the power of God to forgive their sin. In the Gospels, Jesus speaks directly to this point, addressing those who accuse him of suspicious healings, asking whether their own healing practices were any different.

Nonetheless, Jesus had apparently caused some Pietists (see earlier discussion of their background as an extreme offshoot of Jerusalem Pharisees) to question whether he wasn't claiming the prerogative to re-Covenant those with maladies of punishment, inheritors of sin who were being exiled by God, and whose suffering was evidence of their defiled lineages. From his perspective, to the contrary, Jesus was attempting to enable Jews who had strayed from the Covenantal community to return, that is, be restored through Torah education and ritual observance. He does not see what he is doing as "re-Covenanting" individuals whose lineages have become non-Hebrew.

Further observing that the disciples didn't wash before eating, the Pietists challenged Jesus' failure to insist they do so. On the surface, this "hand-washing confrontation" (Mark 7) seems to be of little importance. In fact, as explained earlier, the issue had far deeper roots than has been formerly realized. For historical reasons, though obscure at first glance, the failure to wash their hands was a serious sign to Pietists they possibly had defiled or non-Hebrew lineages. If so, Jesus was re-Covenanting and ordaining the inclusion of his "exiled" followers—an apparent assertion of divine authority.

This then was the mounting suspicion of at least some Pietists who anointed themselves as equal to priests, preparing for God's return: They judged the suspect Northern locals, including Jesus' followers, as lacking the lineage-purity required of the Bridal People to once again be loved as God's Bridal People. In order to preserve their separation from the impure population, the Pietists treated them as a contaminant community avoiding and isolating them from any social interaction. As for Jesus, his efforts to teach and heal met with suspicion that he was claiming authority to supersede Torah with his own brand of Judaism, pretending to messianic identity, by promising the defiled locals a place in God's Kingdom when it commenced. Adding fuel to the fire, was the disciples' proud boast, whispered so he would not hear, that their teacher Jesus was God's son, the King of the Jews, come to usher in His Kingdom. The healings and forgiveness of sin, the signs of his authority to overrule laws of Torah governing the Shabbat were just a taste of what the world would see when he revealed himself.

B. HISTORICAL SEQUENCE OF EVENTS CRITICAL TO JESUS' LAST YEAR

The reader should keep in mind that the following sequence also includes events of lesser consequence to Jesus' fate, which may not always be correct in their temporal order. Whether a specific minor event, such as a given teaching or healing occurred prior to, or after another matters less than establishing the correct causality and chronological sequence of critical, significant events. Those events which are critical to understanding the life and death of Jesus are fully examined in Part II, above, and appear in boldface on this list where Gospel references are provided. Their attestation is based on the particular insight clarifying subsequent critical events which until now were obscured beneath layers of Christianizing midrashic enhancement.

1. *Healing of Simon's mother-in-law.*
2. *Word spreads.*
3. *Healing of a woman on Shabbat.*
4. *Healing of a man with dropsy on Shabbat.*
5. *Dinner at home of congregants: Parable of forgiven tax collector.*
6. ***Healing of leper**–Jesus' wears Jewish ritual fringes. This is the first time some said Jesus claimed divine authority to forgive sin.*
7. *Torah law, as Jesus understood, permits those who are hungry to eat unharvested grain at the edge of a private field on Shabbat or any other day.*
8. *The popular superstition concerning a False Teacher, an emissary of satan (Beelzebul), swirls about.* **Rumors, partly spread by Simon, quote Jesus declaring himself "Master of the Shabbat," and saying, "it was made for him."**
9. **Hand-washing episode: insult and contempt**
10. *Jesus trades insults with the Pietists.*
11. *Jesus explains basics of the law to Simon. (re: Murder, adultery, etc.)*
12. ***Jesus and the disciples attend a Shabbat service in Kfar Nahum. A man screams at Jesus, "I know who you are. You have come to destroy us!"***
    Jesus regards the congregant's wild accusation and hysterical behavior as a sign he is possessed. When he touches the man to exorcise the possible demon, the man collapses. Others in the congregation who know the man, believe he is normal–that Jesus intends to destroy the faithful Jews (not demons!)–and the word/rumors spread that he is an emissary of satan.

[NOTE: Rosh ha-shannah (the New Year) and Yom Kippur (the Day of Atonement) are holidays which Jesus observed, ritually, spiritually and culturally. They were deleted from the Gospels to portray the new messianic time as the sole path to salvation through Jesus, not through Jewish tradition. We may recognize Jesus' participation in the Rosh ha-shannah/ Yom Kippur holidays from the vestiges of his teaching of the Torah laws relating to their observance. Especially on Rosh ha-shannah of the Roman year 31CE soon to end, with a "sabbatical year" commencing, he taught the ritual requirements regarding forgiveness of grudges and debt.]

13. *Parable of king's unforgiving servant. Theme/lesson: Treat others as you would have them treat you (a Torah law). Also: You must forgive others if you expect God to forgive you. (Matthew 18:23-35) John makes speeches against Antipas, accusing the tetrarch of adultery with Herodias.*

    Those Pietists who have garnered favor with Antipas by heralding his adulterous marriage to Herodias are appointed to his ministerial council as a reward for their support. They are called "Herodians."

14. *"Render unto Caesar..." is Jesus' likely sarcasm toward the tax authorities. (Matthew 22:21)*

15. *"Do not lay up for yourselves treasures on earth where moth and rust destroy them." (Matthew 6:19)*

16. *"Make friends with your debtor..." (Matthew 5:25)*

17. *Jesus makes a disparaging reference to "Non-Jews." (Matthew 18:16)*

18. ***Rosh ha-shannah in Nazareth. He goes to his home town from Kfar Nahum with his disciples (following the misguided "exorcism" of a righteous man).***

19. *He replies to those who have heard what happened in Kfar Nahum— and now think he is himself possessed: "You who have heard about Kfar Nahum will say to me, 'Physician heal thyself,'" meaning, "It is you who needs an exorcism!'" (Luke 4:23)*

    The following are central Rosh ha-shannah lessons and would have had special resonance in the year 31-32 CE, the Sabbatical when forgiveness of debt, insults, grievances and an end to arrogance and grudges were commanded in the Torah:

20. *Jesus attends the Nazareth synagogue with his disciples on Rosh ha-shannah. (Luke 4:16)*

21. *"Love your neighbor..." Loosen debt on earth, so God will free you from your debt to Heaven (Torah law). (Mark 12:31)*

22. *"When you pray, don't stand all the time": a criticism of the exhibitionistic Pietists wanting to seem holier than others. (Matthew 6:5)*

23. *"Don't babble when you pray": like non-Jews—or the am-ha-aretz (see Part I for more on their identity). (Matthew 6:7)*

24. *"Judge not lest you be judged..." (Matthew 7)*

25. *Give charity—what you can, and not in a way that advertises your having done so. Mention of Pietists' manner of giving—and shofar blast to signal they have made a donation. (This is specifically related to Rosh ha-shannah, as that is the occasion when the shofar would have been sounded in the synagogue). (Matthew 12:44)*

26. *Jesus reads from scripture in the synagogue on Rosh ha-shannah. (Luke 4:17)*

27. *Jesus challenges those accusing him of being an emissary of satan: "How can satan be against satan?" In other words, would I be exorcising demons if I was from satan? (Mark 3:26)*

28. *Rejected, he says, "No man is a prophet in his own home." (Matthew 13:57)*

29. *Outside the Nazareth synagogue, on Rosh ha-shannah, he reacts to his mother and brothers who try to stop his "mad behavior," saying, "This is not my family..." (Mark 3:33)*

30. ***Jesus tells Pietists (referring to his disciples): "Every good tree bears good fruit..." meaning his disciples' good deeds prove they are legitimate Hebrews. They don't need to prove they have a pure family tree. (Matthew 7:20)***

    [Note: This is a strong rabbinic tradition, echoed in the somewhat later Babylonian Talmud. "Gemilut hasidim" is considered an identifying trait of the Jewish people; (Babylonian Talmud, Yebamot

79a); if one has compassion for others, one is to be considered as though one is a Jew.]

the son of man

31. *Jesus uses the term "sons of men"–indicating he sees himself as a "son-of-man" in the human sense, like the others to whom he is referring. (Mark 3:28)*

32. *Speaking to the Pietists he says, "If you would judge the splinter in the eye of others, first take the plank out of your own eye." (Matthew 7:5)*

33. *He cautions his disciples that to follow the Pietists who suggest they would make better teachers,"will be the blind leading the blind..." (Luke 6:39)*

34. *Again warning his disciples, he says, "You are the salt of the earth –but if you leave me, you will be like salt that has lost its taste." (Matthew 5:13)*

    Although Yom Kippur occurs ten days after Rosh ha-shannah, and precedes Sukkot (the Feast of Booths) by five days, Jesus' teachings and episodes relating to Sukkot begin shortly after the Nazareth synagogue episode, just after Rosh ha-shannah.

35. *On the way to Cana for the wedding, Jesus appears to be still aggravated that his disciples were tempted to go off to study with Pietist rabbis, and points to the fragile Sukkot (Feast of Booths) huts being built. "A house built on sand will collapse in the wind..." (Matthew 7:24-27)*

The Cana wedding

36. *Jesus fills the water purification vessels with wine. People joke sarcastically that he has turned the water to wine (replicating the Sukkot ritual conducted by the High Priest at the Jerusalem Temple). His mother is upset because his acting "crazy" will prevent him from getting married. "Shetuki is shetufi"–a popular saying meant one who cannot identify his father acts like a crazy person. When his mother warns him, that if he kept on, "you will never find anyone to marry," he replies, "It is not my time to get married." But he has,*

just about then, become aware, seemingly from her manner, that Joseph is not his father. Adding to his deep dispair is the realization Mary had given birth to him from an act of adultery. Whoever his father may have been, his lineage is contaminated by sin.

37. *The adulteress brought by Pietists before Jesus as a test to see how he would judge her. (John 7:53-8:11)*

    (Note: This is an odd scene. As it is described in the Gospel, one may wonder what the Pietists are trying to prove. Certainly it can't be that Jesus is "soft" on adulterers. His teaching contains only the harshest rebuke of infidelity. Though my assumption that the "adulteress" symbolized Jesus' mother is conjecture, the likelihood based on context is persuasive.)

    Instead of condemning her, Jesus, says, "Let him who has not sinned cast the first stone," essentially repeating his Torah teaching, "Do not judge or you will be judged."

    The earthshaking reality that he is progeny of an unknown man is evoked by the vision of his mother (hypothetical) as an adulteress after the Cana revelation.

    "Temptation" on the Jerusalem Temple mount

38. ***"Temptation on the Mount" is Jesus' near suicide at the outset of the Feast of Booths (Sukkot) festival.*** *His dispair is the result of believing he had given voice to his possibly satanic, unknown father by exalting himself in the eyes of his disciples. Blaming himself for a dark inclination to encourage their reverence of him as ruler over Torah's laws and traditions, he is about to throw himself down the cliff when he decides to seek John's lineage-purification immersion (baptism).*

    Jesus' baptism by John

39. ***In a desperate effort to be cleansed of his lineage sin, as well as unintended self-exaltation, Jesus' seeks baptism by John.***

    The immersion was a ritual bath of pilgrims to cleanse sin from their lives, both ancestral lineage-contamination and present transgressions. Jesus spends the festival in a sukkah (ritual booth/hut) and invites several disciples he meets in the area to "come see where I am staying." (John 1:38-39)

40. **Don't think I wish to abolish Torah...**

Jesus declared, according to Matthew 5:17-19 (reconstructed according to prior analysis): **Think not that I am here with you to abolish the Torah and prophets. I am not with you to abolish them but to teach you to keep them. For truly I say to you heaven and earth will pass away before a yud or tittle will pass away from the Torah.**

Therefore, whoever breaks the least of these commandments will be called least in the Kingdom of Heaven. But whoever does them and teaches them will be called great in the Kingdom of Heaven.

Because Jesus' seeming reverence for Torah is of critical significance, the prior discussions provide a complete textual analysis of the Gospel passage, discerning what Jesus said and what he meant.

41. *More authentic teachings:*
    a. *If a house is cleansed of demons, seven will return. (Matthew 12:44-45)*
    b. *If somebody needs your tunic, give him your coat. (Matthew 5:40)*
    c. *Do not ask repayment of money given as charity. (Luke 6:30)*
    d. *Treat others as you would have them treat you. (Luke 6:31)*
    e. *"It is easier for a camel to pass through the eye of a needle, than for a rich man to enter the Kingdom of God." (Matthew 25:13) Various of Jesus' teachings which likely followed the Sukkot of his near-suicide:*
    f. *Jesus says: "Beware of false prophets..." (Matthew 7:15)*
    g. *"A sound tree produces good fruit..." (Matthew 7:17)*
    h. *"Ask and it will be given to you..." (Matthew 7:7)*

42. *JOHN'S ARREST*

To stop John's public denunciation of his adulterous "marriage" to Herodias, his living half-brother's (Philip's) wife, undivorced according to Torah law, the tetrarch Antipas accuses John of sedition for creating popular support for Aretas' incursion.

43. *News of John's arrest reaches Jesus.*

44. *Simon apparently continues to spread word that Jesus is the "Holy one of God."*

    (Note: To say he was the "Holy one of God," was the same as saying he was "King of the Jews"–inasmuch as the messiah was to be a successor to King David. We ascertain Simon promoted the idea of Jesus as King of the Jews from two Gospel sources: the acclamation of the crowd following his eulogy to John, and Simon's own admission to Jesus. See detailed analysis and Gospel references in "Simon, who do you say I am?" above.

    Because the Romans ultimately charged Jesus with claiming to be "King of the Jews," Simon's responsibility for publicizing the royal title was especially significant.

45. **The "miracle" of the paralyzed man lowered through the roof.**

    Jesus sought refuge and privacy in a house (inferring from Acts I:20, Matthias' house) after hearing about John's arrest, when a paralyzed man was lowered through a hole broken open in the roof. (Luke 5:18-19)

    Jesus told the afflicted man he could hope to walk again. Then, in an aside to others, said, "It's a lot easier to tell somebody they will walk again than to get them to stand up and go off with their bedding under their arm."

    Jesus could not heal the man and never pretended otherwise. Nor did he ever say he forgave the man's sins, which, if he spoke for God, would have instantly ended his affliction. In other words, Jesus was not claiming divine powers.

    The Gospels ignore the truth, declaring, "Jesus has forgiven the man. He will walk again," a false account intended to prove he was the chosen one of God. Pietists likely heard the false rumor that Jesus himself had made such a claim.

46. *The Hanukkah (Festival of Lights) confrontation. (John 10:22-10:39)*

    Jesus was assaulted by stone-throwing adversaries.

He reacts:

a. *Jesus defends the idea a person can be called a son-of-God without claiming to be divine. It is a characterization, he says which has similar usage in the Psalms (82).*

b. *He affirms that he has broken no Torah law.*

c. *The defaming insult the attackers (Pietists) use to label Jesus and his followers: "No prophet (messiah) will come from the Galilee" and "They are cursed rabble."*

(Note: The so-called "cursed rabble" appear to be the "am ha-aretz" of the north, who were a class of culturally ignorant residents who neither knew or cared about the Torah's laws. Their lifestyles created the suspicion they were not pure Hebrews but had defiled ancestral lineages. (See Part One discussion.)

Because his attackers echoed the charge that he considered himself the son of God, he again felt compelled to end any such perception of him. He would not tolerate the disciples' secret reverence that they exalted him over Torah law and Jewish tradition.

47. *The disciples, anticipating their stature in God's coming Kingdom, raised questions. They wanted to know what would happen when it occurred, who would be part of it, and when it was going to take place.*

48. *Jesus' reply was becoming increasingly guarded as he couched the answers behind parable-like symbols and metaphor. Pietist adversaries were suspicious he considered himself the son of God, and some of them were represented in Antipas' council (the "Herodians"). He wanted to avoid providing them any legal justification for arresting him as they had John. Were he to say anything they might twist, as if he were God's chosen king ushering in the prophesied Kingdom, that could be construed as sedition.*

At this point (the winter, early 32 CE), Antipas still had no personal motive to suppress Jesus' activity. The hostility of the Pietists toward him as a teacher of Torah falsehoods, and even as a claimant to divine authority, hardly reached the level of subversion. Unlike John, who had vilified the tetrarch and his Roman-law wife (Herodias) as adulterers, inciting Galileans to oppose him in any clash with the Nabateans—Jesus had thusfar remained politically uninvolved.

Moreover, he apparently did not anticipate an overthrow of Antipas and spoke of no sudden political upheaval. However, even in talking about "God's Kingdom" Jesus knew he had to be careful not to say it would happen at the expense of Antipas' rule. So his next teachings were guarded by symbolic allusion.

49. *"This is what the Kingdom is like: A man throws seed and it grows at night." (Mark 4:26-27)*

50. *"It is like a mustard seed, growing from a small seed into the biggest bush..." (Mark 4:31)*

51. *51.When will it occur? "Nobody knows when it will occur except God." (Matthew 24:36)*

52. *Who will be included? "It is like sowing seeds and some fall on rocky soil and do not grow, some on good soil." Those who had the capacity to appreciate Torah would grow and become part of the Kingdom.*

53. *As his teaching failed to take root in the disciples, Jesus became frustrated and critical of them. Not only did he compare them to rocky soil, but in another parable, to leaven. "Three parts flour to one part leaven..." (Matthew 13:33)*

    Jesus had begun to treat some among them in a patronizing manner, even as others did—as am ha-aretz: ignorant locals with dubious origins, likening them to rocky soil for his teaching, with ears that didn't hear, or as leaven he was attempting to mix with Hebrew society.

54. *Though his effort to restore them to the Covenantal fold was wavering, he reassured the disciples they might return to the Jewish "family" and be warmly welcomed. To help them understand, he told a story about an outcast member of a Jewish family who repented and was received with a great feast when he came home.*

Parable of the sinful son who returned to the family. *(Luke 15:11-15:32)*

(Note: This is often referred to as the parable of the "Prodigal Son" and is discussed under Jesus' Covenantal restoration parables, above.)

55. *When they became confused by his metaphors, he became irritated and said, "Can't you understand parables?" But seeing malevolent eavesdroppers were listening to his every word, he only explained them in private.*

    Pietists following him around had an agenda to catch him saying something they could take to the authorities as evidence of his causing a public disturbance. As confrontations increased, their purpose took a dangerous turn. Aware John had been arrested for saying Herodias, the tetrarch's wife, was an adulteress, they sought a way to trap Jesus into saying the same thing, so they asked him about divorce and whether it was permissible (having themselves born the brunt of his rebuke as adulterers).

    And, he tells them: "to divorce your wife in order to be with another woman who has caught your eye, is adultery. And your wife who is sent away under such circumstances is not divorced, so that she too becomes guilty of adultery by finding a new man she calls her husband. If your eye would cause you to divorce your wife, I tell you to gouge it out, rather than be condemned to hell and gehinnom." (Matthew 5:28-32)

56. *The Pietists pose a riddle. If Jesus answers as they expect, they will use his words to show he considered the tetrarch's marriage adulterous. (Matthew 22:24-22:34)*

    The riddle asks what if a husband dies and the widow marries his brother only to meet them both in heaven? Was the second marriage adulterous? It was similar to what Herodias had done—divorcing Antipas' brother Philip in order to marry him. Philip, at this time, was still alive—but Roman law empowered women to seek a divorce, which she did. The Pietists supported her wedlock to Antipas, though it was contrary to Jewish law, because she was a descendant of the royal Hebrew line of Hashmoneans (Macabees). The Pietists hoped, therefore, that she would be made queen by the Romans.

57. *Jesus' response to the riddle (seeing through their ominous intent to have him imply the tetrarch's marriage was adultery): "There*

is no such thing as marriage in heaven. People become much like the angels..."

58. *Jesus was quick to recognize their objective: to get him to say something similar to John's pronouncements so he too could be arrested.*

    Therefore, he challenges their self-righteousness, asserting their lineage is tainted and sinful.

    They are, he says, defiled by the murder of the prophet Zechariah, carried out by their forbears. What right did sinners such as they, with lineages stained by a prophet's blood, have to provide testimony against John?

59. *He uses a parable, told as riddle, to show the innocence of John—and to blame the Pietists for bearing false witness against him, resulting in his incarceration.*

    The parable: (Matthew 21:28-21:32)

    Two sons were asked by their father to help in the field. One said no, but had a change of heart and went. The other said yes, but didn't bother.

    Who was the righteous son?

    Their answer was that it was the son who said no, but later repented and went to help his father.

    "Therefore," Jesus said, "That son was like those who came to John—sinners of all kinds who were changing their ways. But for what John did, you have accused him of wrongdoing and had him arrested."

60. *Jesus then declared:"You would strain out a gnat and let in a camel." John was the gnat, a small annoyance, while the Nabatean warrior king, Aretas, was a genuine threat (intending to attack Antipas for having sent away, or caused his daughter to flee, in order to replace her with Herodias). Aretas was pictured on his coins with his camel and was certainly the one compared by Jesus to John as a camel to a "gnat." (Matthew 23:24)*

61. *On the continuing trek northward, Jesus' entourage enters the vicinity of Samaria. (Note: Samaria was the original capital city of the northern kingdom,"Israel." From the late 10th century to*

721BCE, the era when the country was divided, the separate, Jerusalem-centered kingdom was called "Judah.") In the course of Samaria's history following conquest of the north by Assyria, non-Hebrews were forcibly brought to the region and it evolved into a hybrid society with its own traditions sharply divergent from the Jewish religion. Culturally, the Samaritan society came to be violent toward Hebrews whom they hated for rejecting them as ignorant people with doubtful lineages.

62. *Jesus tells the parable of the "Good Samaritan." (Luke 10:29-10:37)*
    The parable teaches that a Samaritan, too, can be a good person— and compared to an individual who lacks compassion—even a traditional Hebrew—a good Samaritan is more righteous.

63. *Jesus snaps angrily at a disciple: "Who appointed me your judge?" (Luke 12:14)*
    This is an important contra-Christianizing criticism for regarding him as the messiah-king. It is evidence, along with similar contra-Christian pronouncements that Jesus did not see himself as the anointed, "chosen one."

64. *The parable of the rich man who put his "faith" in money, not God.*

65. *A disciple addresses Jesus as, "Good Teacher." Jesus angrily reprimands him for excessive reverence, determined to quash the perception he has divine stature: "Why do you call me 'good?' Only God is good." (Luke 18:19)*
    This too is a contra-Christian pronouncement, similarly intended to stop the disciples from elevating him to a supra-human, messianic level.

66. *Reaching the Galilee, Jesus is met by representatives of three lakeside towns which were his usual "stomping ground": Chorazin, Beit Zaida, and Kfar Nahum. They refuse to permit him to enter their region.*

67. *He reacts, declaring: "Woe to you Chorazin..." (Matthew 11:21)*

68. *Turning to his disciples, he indicates they should go off on their own. (Matthew 10)*
    (Note: In the Gospels this is known as "The sending away of the twelve" and is interpreted as granting authority to his disciples

to carry on in his name, a motif which was amplified after his death, granting to the disciples and apostles authority to carry on his mission to save mankind.)

69. *Jesus assures them they are equal to other Hebrews—a reassurance as they are about to go off. It is presented in the form of a Covenantal restoration parable of the last laborer who will be paid the same as the first—though he has not worked as long in the vineyard. (Matthew 20:1-20:16)*

70. *Jesus bids them farewell and retreats.*
   Word reaches Jesus that John has been executed.

Jesus' eulogy for John

(The reader may wish to note that this eulogy appears in this study for the first time, and should be regarded as a major advance in New Testament analysis.)

71. ***Jesus and Matthias make their way to the Sea of Galilee, and approach the crowd gathering to mourn John. Jesus remarks, "They are like sheep without a shepherd."***

72. ***Those present include Jesus' disciples whom "he sent away" and have now come to the funeral gathering. They greet him and report there are people doing exorcisms in his name. Impervious to the messianic compliment, he says, "At least the one doing that doesn't hate me..."***

73. ***Jesus, seeing the crowd includes his Pietist adversaries, among them Herodians who testified against John, aims his remarks at them:***

   a.   ***"One greater than John has never been born..."***

   b.   ***"Did you expect him to wear clothes like those worn by one living in a palace?"***

   c.   ***"Did you expect him to bend like a reed in the wind?" (like the Herodians who supported Antipas no matter what he did).***

   d.   ***"The Kingdom is not coming with signs..."***

e. *"A woman may not divorce her husband..." This was what John had said, blaming Antipas and Herodias for an adulterous marriage since her husband had never given her a divorce. (Only the husband could grant a Jewish divorce.)*

74. *Jesus wades through choppy water towards the disciples' boat.*

   (Note: This was later legendized in the Gospels as the miracle of walking on water.)

   As he goes, the gathering hails him, "King of the Jews," and follows him, grabbing at his clothing. Freeing himself from their grasp, he clambers aboard the boat.

75. **Jesus becomes a fugitive from Antipas**

   The "Miracles": feeding the multitude loaves of bread and fish, walking on water, calming rough waves.

76. *Herodians (Pietist members of Antipas' council) report Jesus has been hailed King of the Jews—and has declared a woman could not divorce her husband (making Herodias an adulteress). Chuza, a worker in the tetrarch's palace, tells his wife Joanna to get word to Jesus: Antipas has labelled him "another John" and intends to do to him what he did to John.*

77. *She brings the message to Jesus, on the shore of Magdala where they beached the boat to eat and rest: "Antipas wants to kill you."*

78. *Jesus replies: "Tell that fox that I am leaving his region."*

79. *Aware from what Joanna says that the Herodians have accused him of defaming Herodias, Jesus warns his disciples: "Beware the yeast of the Herodians and Pietists..." Even more ominously, Jesus suspects the Herodians have reported that he was hailed, "King of the Jews," which could be labelled evidence of sedition.*

80. *The idiomatic usage, where yeast was an impurity (distortion) giving "rise" to false accusations, escapes his disciples. They think he is referring to bread, because they are hungry. Mary, who lives in Magdala, brings a basket of bread and fish.*

(Note: The Gospels will Christianize this as the miracle of loaves and fish.)

81. *As they are soon to depart, Jesus says: "Foxes have holes...but I have nowhere to lay my head...go your own way."*

82. *Simon: "Where else shall we go but with you?"*

83. *Rowing north, they are in shallower, more choppy water, approaching the shore in Philip's territory. Jesus jumps out to lighten the boat so it won't be swamped.*

(Note: In the Gospels this will be Christianized as the miracle of calming the storm which threatened the boat.)

84. Walking by themselves, but apparently overheard, Jesus demands, "**Simon, who do you say I am?**"

When Simon answers that people said Jesus was either Elijah or John reborn, Jesus interjects, "**But who do <u>you</u> say I am?**" wanting him to give his own opinion.

Simon answers, 'You are the Holy one of God...'

And Jesus says: "If you continue saying such things about me I will be arrested..." to which Simon replies, "That could never happen to you, lord."

And Jesus, becoming enraged, tells him: "If you keep calling me 'lord,' I will say I never knew you...Walk behind me satan—you are not walking at the side of a god, you are walking at the side of a man..."

This was the first time Jesus knew for certain that Simon had been saying he was King of the Jews.

Jesus upbraiding Simon for calling him, "lord," saying that Simon is speaking with the voice of satan when he exalts him as God's chosen king, has a remarkable postmortem twist: Christianity's Gospel authors explain that Jesus did not want Simon to cause his capture before reaching Jerusalem where God ordained his crucifixion. In this Christianized version, Jesus blesses Simon with the "keys to the Kingdom," making him Peter (foundation of the faith) and Jesus' arbiter of who might enter the saved state on earth.

85. **Jesus' final Passover**
    a. **advance arrangements for the ceremonial meal**
    b. **entry into Jerusalem**
    c. **the meal ("last supper")**
    d. **Judas' betrayal**
    e. **arrest**
    f. **hearing before Caiaphas**
    g. **judgment before Pontius Pilate**
    h. **crucifixion**
    i. **entombment, disappearance**
    j. **reconstructing what actually happened**
    k. **who was Joseph of Arimathea?**

    The group avoids the hostile region of Samaria, wending their way south, coming to the border between Philip's tetrarchy—and the more perilous region under Antipas' rule—the "Decapolis." To avoid notice and possible arrest, Jesus melds with the crowd. Simon later explains his fugitive manner as a determined attempt to fulfill God's plan by dying in Jerusalem, not en route.

86. *Finally, they reach Bethany, where two sisters, Mary and Martha provide hospitality. They are devotees of Jesus.*

    Martha, who serves the meal, is jealous of Mary when she sees her rubbing Jesus' feet with fine oils. He says Martha shouldn't be jealous, but she should still give her sister a good portion. Typically, Simon imputes a transcendental message to Jesus' good-humored words, thinking he must be promising her a good portion in the coming Kingdom.

87. *When Jesus gives instructions to "follow a water carrier to find a room," Simon takes it as evidence of Jesus' omniscience. He is unfamiliar with the routine of water carriers usually entering courtyards where homeowners made matzah and provided space to Passover pilgrims.*

    In Jerusalem during the Passover festival:
    a. *Coins with images of Tyrian gods, or the Roman emperor, were replaced by a money changer who provided silver useable in the Temple area to purchase a lamb.*

b. *A water carrier led them to a house with available space, which they reserved.*

c. *A lamb for the sacrifice was purchased.*

d. *It was slaughtered and taken to the home where space for the meal had been arranged.*

(Note: The apparent deletion of the purchase, sacrifice and eating the lamb from the Gospel account likely was intended to preserve a theological agenda depicting Jesus as the sacrificial "lamb." He could not be considered God's innocent-lamb-sacrifice for mankind's sins if he was eating lamb. Still, the Christianizing version of a Passover meal minus its key food item fails on other grounds. Simply, the Passover lamb was never a sin offering. Quite in contrast to the Yom Kippur sacrifice of a goat, the lamb was a peace offering. Further revealing the strained Christianizing effort to transform the supper into a messianic drama, the Gospel of John places it a day earlier than Passover. Coinciding with Passover's first night, as portrayed in the other Gospels, the lambs had already been slaughtered for the meal.)

Jesus arrives at the Jerusalem gate, and making his way with his disciples continues his wary manner, doing his utmost to avoid recognition.

Later, the Gospel version will assert that Jesus rode on an ass, entering like the King of the Jews (as described by the prophet Zechariah). Matching this moment to the messianic portrayal, adoring crowds threw leafy branches before him and cried out their praise. This imagery is in total disregard of the predominant reality that Jesus, all through the meal and in the garden where he was arrested, spurned notoriety or adulation, and did everything within his power to avoid capture. Turning over the tables of the money changers (as portrayed in the Gospel of John, drawing upon a messianic motif from the prophet Zechariah), was also an absolute impossibility given Jesus' effort to maintain a low profile.

88. **The Passover supper**
    a. *Jesus insists Simon let him wash his feet.*
    b. *As the meal progresses, Jesus says, "One of you who has dipped with me will betray me."*
    c. *When Judas replies, "Is it I?" Jesus answers, "They are your words."*
        The words were a legal formulation used to charge an accuser with bearing false witness.
    d. *Judas departs and does not return.*

89. **The Arrest**
    a. *The supper done, the group departs for the Garden of Gethsemane only a short ways up the Mount of Olives.*
    b. *Simon is honored to be a guard, assuring Jesus nobody will get past him.*
        "I would lay down my life for you," he says. Jesus replies, "before the cock crows to announce morning, you will deny knowing me..."
    c. *Jesus prays to be saved.*
    d. *The arresting officers approach. Judas indicates which one is Jesus by kissing him.*
    e. *Jesus tells them, "If I am the one you are looking for, let these others go..."*

The hearing before Caiaphas, the High Priest.

Simon remains in the exterior courtyard, outside, while "the disciple" (presumably, Matthias, known as a Sanhedrin scribe) is admitted entry.

Asked whether he claims to be the messiah, Jesus replies, "They are your words..." a formulation Caiaphas understood legally accused him of bearing false witness (the same as Jesus addressed to Judas).

Caiaphas is irate that despite their critical remarks, no witnesses will give the testimony necessary to find Jesus guilty. None of the Jews present would say they ever heard Jesus claim to be "King of the Jews." When Caiaphas can't

> ***get Jesus to admit he makes that claim, he finally orders his***
> ***removal for the pre-arranged sentencing by Pontius Pilate.***

90. *As Jesus is brought before Pilate, Simon says to an inquiring officer monitoring those who approached the gate, "I don't know him."*

91. *Jesus is judged by Pontius Pilate*
    Elements of the scene include:
    a. *Interrogation (insincere and reflecting the procurator's amused curiosity more than an interest in justice).*
    b. *Jesus realizes that no matter what he says, his fate has been decided.*
    c. *Antipas joins the scene of Pilate's judgment. It is a debacle mocking Jesus as "King of the Jews." He is forced to wear a royal purple robe, hold a reed scepter, and wear a crown of thorns, while Antipas' retinue bows before him and spits in his face.*
       Pilate defers jurisdiction to Antipas—tetrarch of the region where Jesus lives.
    d. *Jesus is found guilty of sedition—claiming to be "King of the Jews."*
       (Note: As has been explicated earlier, Jesus' actual "offense" was castigating Antipas and his wife as adulterers, married without Herodias having been divorced according to Jewish law. The insult branding her an adulteress echoed John's harangues and Antipas followed up on his threat: He would stop Jesus from taking over for John. What he had done to John, he would do to Jesus.)
       Jesus is led away to be crucified.
       Along the route, the cross is placed on his shoulders and a passing Cyrene is enlisted to help with the lower part as he drags it uphill to Golgotha, the area of crucifixion.

92. *Joseph's servant, Nicodemus, and the "disciple" (Matthias) are witnesses. No other friends, family, disciples or devotees are there. It is Friday, the first day of Passover and Jewish officials and priests are elsewhere, being engaged in the Temple ceremony.*

What Jesus says from the cross:

a. *To (Matthias), who has acquired a shroud somewhat earlier, Jesus says,*

   "Take care of my nakedness."

   (Note: These words in the Gospels were changed to "Take care of my mother." The Greek for "nakedness" and "mother" are very similar. It is owing to this misrepresentation of Jesus' request, that his mother, Mary, has been pictured as present during the crucifixion.)

b. *"Eli, Eli, lama sabachthani." My God, my God—why have you destroyed/killed me?* (Note: The more familiar, alternate translations, "Why have you forsaken me? or, "Why have you abandoned me?" are words Christianized for their messianic, poignant motif, suggesting that even Jesus needs to feel God's Presence at the point of death.)

c. *"It is finished."*

(Note: The Gospels change this to "It is accomplished," Christianizing the crucifixion as a planned occurrence in the unfolding salvation theology.)

93. *(Matthias) and Nicodemus (Joseph's servant) carry the body to the public tomb used for crucified "criminals" and wrap Jesus in a shroud, according to Jewish custom.*

    Concerning the three things Jesus said from the cross:

    1. "God, why have you destroyed/killed me?"

       Comment: Arguably, if Jesus was "in on" the salvation theology, he would have understood he was suffering his fate as necessary and not wonder why God was letting him be murdered. Perhaps owing to this seeming contradiction, the Gospels of Luke and John both omit these words. Yet, their inclusion in the Gospels of Matthew and Mark strongly attest to their historical veracity.

    2. "Take care of my nakedness."

       This was Jesus' request (attributed in this study to Matthias) that he be wrapped in a shroud, and so be buried according to Jewish custom. In the Gospel of John, "nakedness" is changed to "mother" and is then enhanced by the image of Mary standing with Matthias (called the "disciple Jesus loved") at the foot of the cross.

3. "It (my suffering) is finished."
   Only in the Gospel of John, are the words altered to have Jesus say:
   "It is accomplished." The other Gospels omit them entirely. A Christianized change, Jesus is here revealing his crucifixion is "an accomplishment" fulfilling God's design.

94. *Jesus expires after six hours on the cross (on Friday, from nine in the morning until three in the afternoon). He is taken to the nearby public cave-tomb for criminals where "the disciple" (Matthias) and Nicodemus (the servant of Joseph of Arimathea) wrap him in a shroud, covering his nakedness according to Jewish tradition—as he had requested from the cross.*

95. *He is in the tomb 27-39 hours (at least the hours from three in the afternoon Friday, until the end of Shabbat, Saturday at sundown, and probably until late Saturday night or very early Sunday morning).*

96. *Joseph of Arimathea (recognized in this study to be "Joseph of Ir ha-mayteem" (Jesus' nominal father) is accompanied by (his servant) Nicodemus to the cave-tomb and his bloody shroud is removed from his body and folded to the side. His body is covered with aloe, and the folds of the new shroud are filled with myrrh.*

97. *Jesus is taken to a different (or "new") tomb, and interred there.*

C. THE POSTMORTEM PARABLES

Various parables created after Jesus' death, have an apparent function of keeping faith alive that Jesus had been resurrected and was guiding the chosen ones from heaven. Further, they warn the wavering followers of exclusion and punishment.

The parable of the "Ten Bridesmaids" is a prime example (Matthew 25:1-13). The bridesmaids represent the ten disciples (not including either Judas Iscariot, who is gone—or Simon who presides but does not count himself).

The five who "keep their lamps filled with oil" (that is, have faith they will see Jesus' return) are expected to ally themselves with Simon in promulgating the new theology. The other five have doubts God planned the crucifixion and balk at the model of salvation requiring so cruel a death of their beloved teacher. (Interestingly, it seems Simon no longer considers himself a mere "bridesmaid.")

However, the actual identities of the two groups must be labelled conjecture. Reasonable surmise suggests those disciples who were from the same lakeside village, Beit Zaida, may well constitute Simon's most "loyal" five. They were Andrew, Philip, the Zebedees and Thomas, the latter three, likely living in the vicinity. If so, those arrayed in opposition were Simon C'nani, James bar Alpheus, Thaddeus, Matthew and Bartholomew, with Matthias (who had replaced Judas Iscariot), not a bridesmaid because he wasn't chosen by Jesus, but simply "invited" by Simon. Very plausibly he had already been expelled from the group when this parable was authored. Matthew may have ultimately swung over to support Simon, while Philip joined his adversaries.

Another apparently postmortem parable is further evidence that Matthias was expelled from the group of disciples for failing to acknowledge Jesus as the son of God. It is theologically known as the Parable of the Wedding Banquet (Matthew 22:11-14). According to the text, the wedding of "the king's son" is "crashed" by a guest who the king recognizes is an interloper, conspicuously not wearing the proper wedding garment.

As he is thrown out, the king declares, "many are called, but few are chosen." The only disciple "called"—that is, invited, was Matthias, by Simon, to fill the place of Judas Iscariot. The others were "chosen" by Jesus when he was alive. Regarding the "garment," it was a fairly standard symbol of knowledge. Thus, the wedding "garment" would have been the "knowledge" that Jesus was the son of God and was the groom of mankind, a long-time traditional metaphor of the savior's role.

This postmortem "king's-son's wedding" parable was also a warning to those wavering disciples who doubted Jesus' crucifixion was God's plan.

Another postmortem warning parable was quite plausibly directed at James and is known as the Parable of the Pounds (Luke 19:11-19:27). In sum, it tells of a landowner who took a journey. He entrusted several servants with his wealth. One acted differently than the others, hiding it in the ground, rather than investing it. Upon his return, those who invested the wealth (symbolically, spread belief in Jesus) were granted rule over various cities—but the one who failed to add to the buried money, through investment, was told: "All those (like you) who have nothing (symbolically, burying your belief in Jesus)—from you everything will be taken, but to you who have much (that is, wealth as knowledge of Jesus' divine rule) much more will be given!

And, if there is any doubt this particular parable was authored postmortem, the harsh punishment for failing to spread belief in the messianic Jesus leaves no doubt. It states: "As for those enemies of mine who do not want me to be king over them, bring them here and slaughter them in my presence."

Other parables with similar harsh punishments, such as the Parable of the Net (Matthew 13:47-50) are also obvious postmortem warnings to proselytized newcomers, lest they risk their mortal souls by doubting Jesus' heavenly rule.

Finally, a third postmortem genre of parables dramatizes the birth of Christian theology (see Matthew 24:26-24:31 and parallels in related texts). These depict a divine Jesus descending from heaven, a significant precept of early Christian theology, and contain various messianic fables and narrative insertions solely intended to amplify the divine identity of Jesus, with transcendent teachings, miracle healings, and resurrection motifs.

GENERAL REFERENCES

Because the thesis of this study is not based on other interpretations, only a small selection of texts and historical surveys are suggested references.

1. Gospel Parallels, Ed. B.H. Throckmorton, Pub: T. Nelson 1979, Tenn.
2. The New Greek-English Interlinear New Testament
   Trans: Brown and Comfort, Pub: Tyndale House, 1993
3. The Complete Wordstudy Dictionary–New Testament
   Ed: S. Zodhiates, Pub: World, 1992
4. The Apocryphal New Testament, Trans. M.R. James, Pub: Oxford Univ. Press, 1924
5. The Old Testament Pseudepigrapha, Vols. I and II, Ed. J.H. Charlesworth, Pub: Doubleday, 1983
6. The Complete Dead Sea Scrolls in English Trans. G. Vermes, Penguin 2004
7. The Works of Josephus, Trans. W. Whiston, Pub: Hendrickson, 1987
8. The Hebrew Bible, various editions, including:
   Pentateuch and Haftarot, Ed. J.H. Hertz, Pub: Soncino
   Tanakh, Pub: Jewish Publication Society
9. The Talmud, Soncino 1977
10. The Legends of the Jews, L. Ginzberg, Jewish Publication Society, 1968
    Useful histories

11. <u>Compendia Rerum Iudaicarum ad Novum Testamentum</u>, The Jewish People in the First Century, Eds. S. Safrai, M. Stern, D. Flusser, W.C. van Unnik, G. Vermes, others. Pub: Van Gorcum and Company, Amsterdam 1974

12. <u>Pilgrimage at the Time of the Second Temple</u>, S. Safrai (Hebrew) Pub: Am Ha-sefer Press, Israel 1965

13. <u>Fellowship in Judaism</u>, The First century and Today, J. Neusner, Pub: Vallentine-Mitchell, 1963

14. <u>A History of the Jewish People</u>, Ed. H.H. Ben-Sasson, Parts II and III, by H. Tadmore and M. Stern, Pub: Harvard Univ. Press, 1976

15. <u>A History of the Jewish People in the Age of Jesus Christ</u>, E. Schurer, Ediors: G. Vermes, F. Millar, and M. Black, Pub: Edinburgh

16. <u>The World History of the Jewish People</u>, Eds. M. Avi-Yonah and Z. Baras, Vol. 7, The Herodian Period by Avi-Yonah, Klausner, Mantel, Safrai, Schalit, and Stern, Pub: Rutgers Univ. Press, 1975

17. <u>The Quest of the Historical Jesus</u>, A. Schweitzer, Trans. W. Montgomery, 1968

18. <u>The Religion of Jesus the Jew</u>, Geza Vermes, Fortress Press, 1993

Special acknowledgment and appreciation is given to Doubleday and Company's "Reader's Edition of the Jerusalem Bible," New York, 1968 Ed. Alexander Jones for the English translations of occasional phrases and short passages.

Printed in the United States
By Bookmasters